The Great Word Catalogue

The Great Word Catalogue

FUNdamental Activities for Building Vocabulary

Susan Ohanian

HEINEMANN
Portsmouth, NH

Heinemann
A division of Reed Elsevier Inc.
361 Hanover Street
Portsmouth, NH 03801–3912
www.heinemann.com

Offices and agents throughout the world

The author and publisher wish to thank those who have generously given permission to reprint borrowed material:

"A word map for middle school: A tool for effective vocabulary instruction" by Catherine Rosenbaum in *Journal of Adolescent & Adult Literacy* 45(1). Copyright © 2001 by the International Reading Association. Reprinted with permission of the author and IRA. All rights reserved.

"Teaching Ideas. Zooming in and zooming out: Enhancing vocabulary and conceptual learning in social studies" by Janis Harmon and Wanda Hedrick in *The Reading Teacher* 54(2). Copyright © 2000 by the International Reading Association. Reprinted with permission of the authors and IRA. All rights reserved.

Library of Congress Cataloging-in-Publication Data
Ohanian, Susan.
   The great word catalogue : fundamental activities for building vocabulary / Susan Ohanian.
      p. cm.
   Includes bibliographical references.
   ISBN 0-325-00427-7
  1. Vocabulary—Problems, exercises, etc. I. Title.

PE1449 .O345 2002
428'.0076—dc21   2002009731

Editor: Lois Bridges
Production: Vicki Kasabian
Interior design: Joni Doherty
Cover design: Catherine Hawkes/Cat & Mouse
Typesetter: Tom Allen, Pear Graphic Design
Manufacturing: Steve Bernier

Printed in the United States of America on acid-free paper
06 05   02 VP   2 3 4 5

For Lois Bridges.
Anybody who has worked with her knows why.

For Vicki Kasabian.
Not just because she loves cats.

Contents

INTRODUCTION
Let Us Stand by Words

In a provocative essay titled *Standing by Words*, poet-farmer-essayist Wendell Berry noted the link between the disintegration of language and the disintegration of communities. Berry is not complaining about the way teenagers talk but about the *accountability* of language; he points out that when speakers aren't willing to be accountable for their words, not willing to act on what they say, then public responsibility is distorted into public relations.

This language accountability principle is crucial for classrooms. When we stand by our words then certain principles must underlie vocabulary instruction.

1. Children explore the wit, wonder, wisdom, and whimsy of words throughout the day, every day.

2. Teachers realize that memorization of lists of words and definitions is the least effective way of developing a rich vocabulary.

3. Teachers realize that answering vocabulary drills at the end of each chapter of an exciting book (or a dull book) is the second least effective way of developing a rich vocabulary—and is abusive besides.

Standing by words in the classroom means exploring words for today—for the children and their needs—today. We must help children come to words today—in awe and in love—not in obligation for some committee's business plan for tomorrow. Business plans shift in terms. *Standing by words* means we have a constant faith—in the words and in the children who will use them. We can stand by these words because we stand with and for children as we study words together.

Putting Principles into Practice

Here are ten ways you can remind students about wonderful words throughout the day.

1. *Vocabulary Wall.* Start the day by drawing students' attention to wonderful words you've posted on the wall. This can be single phrases or sentences, excerpts from poems, or a word all by itself. You may want to ask students to keep *Wonderful Words* journals, in which they copy these words each day. Over time, what starts as a teacher-required chore evolves into serendipity: lovely little unplanned discoveries, different for every child, significant to all. Over time, students will start volunteering to post wonderful words they have found.

2. *Vocabulary Testimony.* A good way to end a day is to ask for a student to volunteer a reflection about an interesting word encountered that day. This can be a new word or a new look at an old word. For example, noticing the *ant* in *Anthony* causes young readers to see an old word differently, while noting the *ant* in *jubilant* might well mean encountering a new word.

3. *Arguing for Words.* Provide ongoing opportunities for focused investigation of words. Invite students to choose an "important" word in a play, poem, or story they've just read, and to provide an argument for convincing others of its importance.

4. *Question Box.* Invite students to put questions about words in a box and to become words sleuths, volunteering to find answers.

5. *Expanding Horizons.* Invite ESL students to teach words in their languages. Post some common words such as *mother, father, home* in many languages. Encourage students to come up with a list of basic words, words we can't do without. Look for commonalities and differences in these words in various languages.

6. *Pop-Up Words.* Invite students to create a pop-up card with a word surprise for a classmate, a member of the school staff, or someone special in the community.

7. *Word Collages.* Invite students to create a word collage to express an important idea such as joy, friendship, fear, or other abstractions of their choice.

8. *Word Games.* Invite students to teach a word game to someone they know outside school.

9. *Word Play.* Invite students to create word cartoons that involve puns or some other play on language; provide space in the classroom to display their work.

10. *Trying Out Words.* Encourage students to mark and share new words they try out in their own writing.

Doing all this—and more—means that we will stand up for children's language infatuation rather than lie down for their indoctrination.

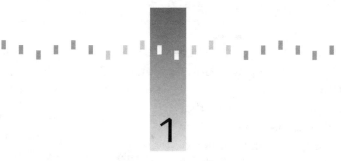

1

Growing Vocabulary the Natural Way

"Well," said Owl, "the customary procedure in such cases is as follows."
"What does Customoney Proceedcake mean?" said Pooh.
"For I am a Bear of Very Little Brain, and long Words bother me."
—A. A. Milne

Unlike Pooh, "Children like a fine word occasionally," Beatrix Potter pointed out when her publisher objected to the appearance of *soporific* in the opening of *The Tale of the Flopsy Bunnies*. And when Chris, who starts every day by announcing how much he hates reading, encounters *soporific*, it stops him cold in his tracks. "What is this word?" He demands, jabbing the page. And I tell him. On the spot. At that moment, for that kid, getting back to the story is what is important. When Chris returns to his desk, he tells Joey about soporific. And they try it out a few times, liking the way it sounds and the way it feels on their tongues. Six weeks later, during the hour-long sustained silent reading that begins our day, Chris puts eleven little Potter books into three piles on his desk while he reads a book of Jack Prelutsky's poems. I notice that he runs his fingers along their small, smooth covers as he reads. Later in the day, Jesse, repeating third grade with an attitude, demands that Chris give up *The Tale of Squirrel Nutkin* because he wants to copy the book into his vocabulary notebook. The whole book. His classmates are dumbfounded. "I like the way the words feel," smiles Jesse, the tough guy of third grade.

"Yeah, but you could just copy some of them," advises Chris. "Not all the *and*s and

*the*s." Jesse stands firm that he wants all of them in his notebook.

Teaching vocabulary is like teaching everything else—figuring out when to step in and offer a definition, when to push and prod the student to figure it out for himself. Most times good readers don't stop to ask about the meaning of a word they don't know. They keep on reading. Sometimes when they ask, a teacher just tells them; other times she tries to nudge them into a strategy that will help them figure it out. There are no rules—except that neither students nor teachers should worry about every undefined word. Nor should teachers worry about giving away definitions without first forcing students to struggle over them. What's more, research shows us students shouldn't even worry about a large percentage of these undefined words, because words have a way of returning again and again. And it's these repeated encounters that build vocabulary.

An ongoing give-and-take exists between vocabulary development and reading comprehension. This is both the good news and the bad news: In order to make sense of what we read, we have to know the meanings of most of the words we encounter. But it's the words we don't know in these encounters that add to our word stock.

Researchers tell us that school-aged children learn as many as three thousand words per year, an average of eight words a day for the most voracious word learners. Most of that learning is incidental—that is, it takes place in the process of reading, listening, and talking. No direct instruction involved. Studying words one by one, or in weekly lists, can account for only a small fraction of the words that children need to know.

If all children learned new words incidentally at this phenomenal rate, all we would have to do is support extensive reading of wonderful books. However, a host of factors, such as learning disabilities and environmental opportunities, create huge gaps in vocabulary acquisition. Beside the child who learns eight words a day sits another who learns just two. As students move through school, the disparities are magnified to the point that the vocabulary of a third grader who's a voracious reader may be equal to that of a senior who reads with reluctance and difficulty.

How Children Learn New Words

In *The Book of Learning and Forgetting*, noted researcher Frank Smith observes, "Since birth, children have been learning new words at the rate of two thousand per year, without conspicuous effort or organized instruction—and without any forgetting." Smith reminds us, "We can learn without effort if we are interested in what we are doing (or in what someone else is doing)."

The research on vocabulary growth is overwhelming, and the advice from those identified with more holistic teaching agree with those identified with more direct instruction: Children acquire vocabulary by reading—and being read to.

■ The single most important activity for building the knowledge required for eventual success in reading is reading aloud to children. (Anderson, Hiebert, et al. 1985)

■ Children who read for pleasure acquire a large vocabulary. They do this involuntarily and without conscious effort. (Krashen 1993)

■ Impressive experimental results show that second-language learners and native English speakers who read more outside of school have better reading comprehension and vocabulary skills. (McQuillan 1998)

■ Most theorists agree that the bulk of vocabulary growth during a child's lifetime occurs indirectly through language exposure rather than through direct teaching. (Cunningham & Stanovitch 1998)

■ What is needed to produce vocabulary growth is not more vocabulary instruction but more reading. (Nagy 1988)

■ Good libraries—not basals, not test prep—raise test scores. Research shows a strong correlation between school library quality, including number of books and number of certified librarians, and reading test scores. (Krashen 1996; Lance 1994)

■ Vocabulary expansion through reading is about ten times more efficient than vocabulary instruction. (Nagy, Anderson, & Herman 1987)

■ Vocabulary learning takes place when students are immersed in words. (Blachowicz & Fisher 1996)

■ The single most important thing a teacher can do to promote vocabulary growth is to increase students' volume of reading. (Nagy 1988)

■ Read, read, read. (Burke 1999)

It can't get any clearer than this. And yet, the mythology supporting vocabulary drill of isolated words persists. In September 2001, the *Washington Post* profiled an English teacher who, the reporter said, "takes vocabulary seriously." The proof? "Her students get a workbook containing three hundred words and exercises to complete sentences and hunt for synonyms." The president of

William H. Sadlier Inc. reports that sales of Sadlier-Oxford's vocabulary workbooks have increased 15 percent in each of the past two years. Thirteen-year-old Joanne Lagratta, who won the National Spelling Bee by spelling *inappetence* and *antipyretic*, showed another way. Joanne told a television reporter that she didn't study a dictionary or word lists. How did she acquire such word competence? "I read all the time," Joanne reported, adding that she liked to read "some books over and over again."

Fostering Literacy Epiphanies

Both the eight-word-a-day children and the two-word children learn the majority of new words in the context of rich, meaningful use of language, so the teacher's classroom commitment must be to provide time and resources for wide independent reading. This includes time to read, a continually expanding supply of attractive reading materials, and opportunities for sharing, questioning, reflecting, and celebrating words. To give a boost to those students whose vocabularies seem weak, we look for ways to help them become skillful at using strategies for learning new word meanings independently. A traditional method has been to ask children to choose unfamiliar words from their reading and record these words in vocabulary journals or writing notebooks. Too often, this becomes a rote exercise, little better than filling in workbook pages.

Remember that the goal is for students to become fascinated by words, *not* for students to fill in lots of pages in a vocabulary notebook. Often, less is more. Fascination with one word can cause an explosion in interest in many words. Cindy, one of the most reluctant readers in a class identified as the worst readers in third grade, had an impressive ability to scowl her way through sustained silent reading: Arms folded, body stiff, her scowl deepened every time she turned a page. But one day she turned a page, did a

Research Note

Richard Allington's research shows that students in high-achieving, high-poverty schools spend an enormous amount of time reading and writing. Kids in low-achieving schools spend lots of time being drilled and doing vocabulary volcano activities.

double take and turned it back, staring at the page. She ran her finger along a line of text. Then she came rushing over to me. "Look at this! *Cook* is in *cookie*. That's probably why they call it cookie—because the cook cooked it!" For Cindy this was an etymological revelation on par with the deciphering of the Rosetta stone.

That one encounter turned Cindy into a reader. From that day on, she looked at words as something that could both surprise her and give her pleasure. She joined the group with an Amelia Bedelia mania, which hooked her into homophones. Cindy set herself the task of learning to spell a long string of homophones so she could fill her daily notes to me with jokes, commenting, "If you spell it wrong you ruin the joke."

Every day I could look forward to a linguistic tour de force invented by Cindy. Katherine Paterson observes that books give children "life and growth and refreshment." Children give us back these very same things—if we let them.

At the end of each year I could look back on many such literacy epiphanies of rotten readers who swore they hated books and who were transformed by a special word or turn of phrase. Yes, they came to love whole books, but most often it was a single word that worked the transformation. Surprising to me, I missed this moment for Leslie, a deaf child to whom I gave more of my heart than any other child. I thought I knew just about all there was to know about Leslie's linguistic journey, and certainly I knew of her many literacy loves, but I learned about her special moment of reading revelation years later, when she phoned me from college, asking if I thought it would be a good idea for her to change her major from architecture to teaching. "I need something that's more people-oriented," she confided. Leslie also told me that seeing her niece's copy of an Amelia Bedelia book brought third-grade memories rushing back. "I worked so hard to understand that book," she said. "The other kids were laughing because Amelia planted light bulbs. But I would have done the same thing. I didn't know there were two kinds of bulbs. More than that, I didn't know that words could mean more than one thing." Leslie didn't want to let on to her classmates—or her teacher—that she didn't get the jokes, so she laughed when the other kids laughed but secretly studied the books and taught herself to understand the multiple meanings of words.

It is humbling to realize I missed something so important. It is reassuring to realize that when you trust kids and books, good things happen without your stage-managing. Teachers are directly responsible for only a small part of what children learn; this is why it is so crucial that we create environments that are conducive to kids learning on their own.

Providing frameworks for student explo-

ration is, of course, an honored teacher strategy for helping students become independent. These days the teacher is under more pressure than ever to remind herself of the huge difference between busywork and learning. Even children who already have rich vocabularies benefit from making explicit some of the strategies they use in figuring out unfamiliar words. Shared reading, done by a skilled reader while students follow along in the text, provides a good opportunity for practice. As children encounter words they don't know, they mark them with Post-Its or other slips of paper. After the reading and discussion, the teacher asks for a volunteer to play Word Sleuth (see next page). The volunteer chooses a word, writes it on the overhead, board, or chart tablet, and reads aloud the sentence. The teacher asks a series of questions that provide scaffolding for the reader's attempts to use word parts, phonics, and context clues to decode the word and get at its meanings. Other volunteers go through the same process with their own words.

The Word Sleuth activity gives students opportunities to practice word sleuth skills that have been demonstrated in class. Making such procedures a weekly part of class routines will teach and reinforce strategies that readers can apply in independent reading.

Creating Relationships to Foster Vocabulary Acquisition

Vocabulary development comes not from acquiring lists of discrete information but from word relationships. We understand new words by linking them to what we already know. Making word relationships visible can be

Student: Word Sleuth

When you come across an interesting or intriguing word you'd like to know, use your skills to see what clues you can find to figure out its meanings.

1. Write the word: _____

2. Write the sentence you found it in:_____
    _____

3. Does the sentence give any clues to the word's meaning? If so, write these clues
    here: _____
    _____

4. Does the word contain any prefixes or suffixes that you recognize? If so, write them
    here: _____

5. Do you know any other words that have the same root or base word? If so, write
    them here: _____

6. Does your knowledge of the topic in general provide information to help you figure
    out this word?

Now make your best guess about the meaning of the word, and then check your guess by consulting a knowledgeable person or a dictionary.

Student: Finders

As you read books, stories, poems, magazines, newspapers, and so on, copy some words you don't know and the sentences in which they appear. Aim for at least ____ new words each week. Choose words that interest or intrigue you. Also consider words that are familiar or that you might have heard before although you aren't sure what they mean. For each word you choose, do the following:

- Write the sentence the word appears in, being careful to spell the target word correctly.
- Use your knowledge of word parts and context clues to make a guess about the word's meaning, and write it down.
- Ask a knowledgeable person or consult a dictionary to check your answer. Write the correct definition if your guess wasn't on target.
- Did anything about what you learned about the word surprise you? Please write a note about this!

helpful. Graphic organizers, semantic webs, and pictorial elements can help students link concepts, experiences, and words. Relying on associations and connections rather than memorization, organizers offer different ways for students to see and use information. These graphic devices not only organize meanings, they also help organize memories. And they also make the learning active if students are involved in discussing what has been organized. Graphic organizers help everybody but are especially useful for helping low-achieving students comprehend nonfiction material. The group discussion of these organizers is especially helpful to students with vocabulary weaknesses. Research shows that without this discussion, the organizers aren't of much use.

Word Mapping

Researcher Susan Carey distinguishes between *fast mapping*, in which children encounter words briefly and form only cursory notions about what they mean, and *extended mapping*, which takes place over time, after multiple encounters with the word, and results in deeper understandings of the word's meanings. A fascinating outgrowth of Carey's research is her hypothesis that children may be working with as many as sixteen hundred word mappings simultaneously.

Writing in the *Journal of Adolescent and Adult Literacy*, Catherine Rosenbaum reports that word mapping is a daily routine for her middle schoolers. She describes how she introduced the methodology:

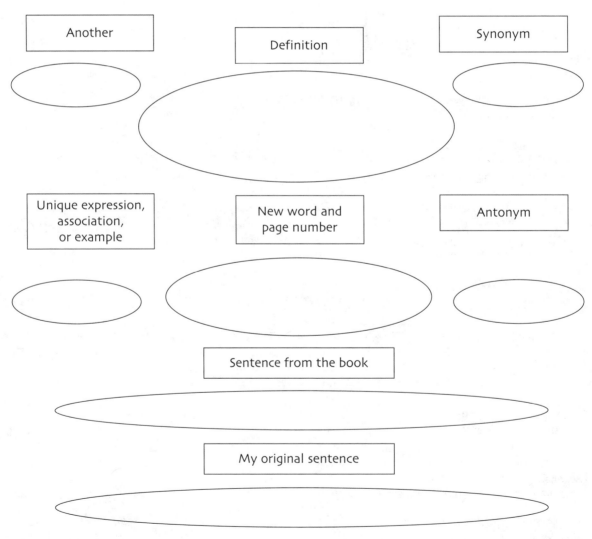

Figure 1. Word map

I listed on the overhead projector a short list of words from the first chapter in the novel we were about to read, *Later, 'Gator* (Yep 1995), and modeled how to map one word for the students. Then I read the chapter out loud while the students followed in paperbacks. When I finished, I asked the students to identify the most difficult word on the list for me to model with the map again. Following my second demonstration, each student mapped one of the remaining words from the list, choosing a fairly familiar one. [See Figure 1]

Conceptual Frameworks

In "Zooming In and Zooming Out: Enhancing Vocabulary and Conceptual Learning in Social Studies," Janis Harmon and Wanda Hedrick also offer a technique for "teaching vocabulary within a conceptually driven framework." They advocate using this technique "judiciously during major shifts in topics that may occur once or twice in a unit of study." Figure 2 shows a lesson used by a fifth-grade teacher to discuss the important vocabulary concept of *artifacts*. Before they read a passage containing the term, children brainstorm what they know about artifacts. Then they read the passage, finding support for what they know and also finding new information. They may fill out a fact sheet with new information as they read. Small groups then decide on three important facts about artifacts they've found in their reading

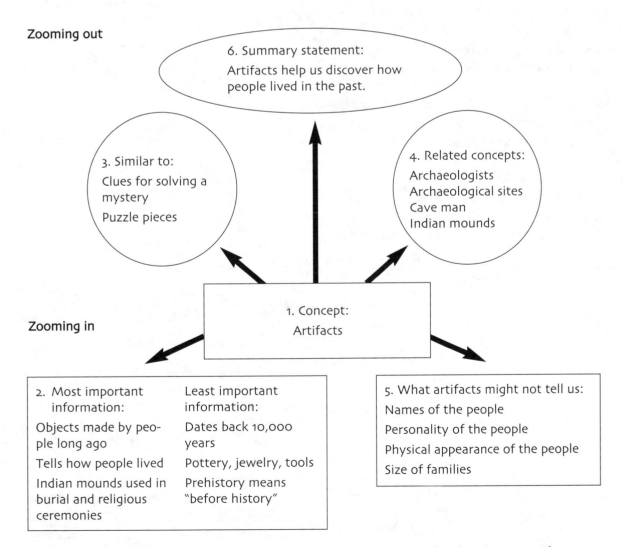

Figure 2. Visual representation of the vocabulary information display for the concept *artifacts*

as well as three facts that are not as important. As the authors observe, the ability to discriminate between significant and trivial information is an important and sophisticated study skill, one requiring lots of practice.

Graphic Organizers

All of the following organizers show a relationship between synonyms and antonyms, but the arrays are very different. Encourage students to find graphic organizers that work well for them. Encourage them to change formats to suit themselves. If graphic organizers become just one more fill-in-the-blank item, then their usefulness is questionable. Organizers can be a way to help students to see cause and effect relationships and sequences in nonfiction material. It is crucial to keep in mind that this isn't just a visual display of information but mainly a means for students to draw on their own background knowledge. Drawing an ant to represent *minute* and an elephant to represent *enormous* does more for a fifth grader's ability to remember a definition than putting the words on sun rays or circles.

LINEAR ARRAYS

A linear array can be presented as a puzzle. Using the example above, challenge students to get from *minute* to *enormous* in four steps.

SUN

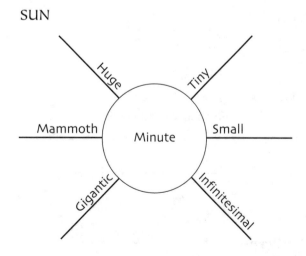

Research Note

Talk is a crucial element in semantic mapping. Summarizing research, Stephen Stahl reports in *Vocabulary Development*, "An individualized mapping procedure, in which students studied maps on their own, did not work as well as a group procedure."

CLUSTERS

This is the same principle as the sun rays but some students prefer this arrangement. Obviously, it doesn't matter what the organizer looks like. What matters is that it helps individual students.

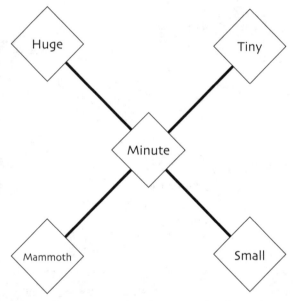

Web Watch

A variety of graphic organizers are available on the Internet. Two useful sites are *www.sdcoe.k12.ca.us/score/actbank/torganiz.htm* and *www.ncrel.org/sdrs/areas/issues/students/learning/lr1grorg.htm*.

Be a Word-Borrower

Here are the ten most popular languages, the countries where they are spoken, and the number of people speaking them (Grimes 1996). Note: Many of the languages listed are technically dialects, not separate languages. They are listed separately because they differ from each other enough to be mutually unintelligible. You can find the top fifty languages at *www.infoplease.com/ipa/A0774735.html*.

1. **Chinese (Mandarin), 885 million**: Brunei, Cambodia, China, Indonesia, Malaysia, Mongolia, Philippines, Singapore, South Africa, Taiwan, and Thailand

2. **Spanish, 332 million**: Andorra, Argentina, Belize, Bolivia, Chile, Colombia, Costa Rica, Cuba, Dominican Republic, Ecuador, El Salvador, Eq. Guinea, Guatemala, Honduras, Mexico, Nicaragua, Panama, Paraguay, Peru, Spain, Uruguay, United States, and Venezuela

3. **English, 322 million**: Australia, Botswana, Brunei, Cameroon, Canada, Eritrea, Ethiopia, Fiji, the Gambia, Guyana, Ireland, Israel, Lesotho, Liberia, Malaysia, Micronesia, Namibia, Nauru, New Zealand, Palau, Papua New Guinea, Samoa, Seychelles, Sierra Leone, Singapore, Solomon Islands, Somalia, South Africa, Suriname, Swaziland, Tonga, United Kingdom, United States, Vanuatu, Zimbabwe, and many Caribbean states

4. **Bengali, 189 million**: Bangladesh, India, and Singapore

5. **Hindi, 182 million**: India, Nepal, Singapore, South Africa, and Uganda

6. **Portuguese, 170 million**: Brazil, Cape Verde, France, Guinea-Bissau, Portugal, São Tomé, and Príncipe

7. **Russian, 170 million**: China, Israel, Mongolia, Russia, and United States

8. **Japanese, 125 million**: Japan, Singapore, and Taiwan

9. **German (Standard)**: Austria, Belgium, Bolivia, Czech Republic, Denmark, Germany, Hungary, Italy, Kazakhstan, Liechtenstein, Luxembourg, Paraguay, Poland, Romania, Slovenia, and Switzerland

10. **Chinese (Wu), 77.2 million**: China

Capitalize on students' interest in foreign words by asking them to search out words in their own families and neighborhoods. Come up with a class agreed-upon list of twenty common words; words for *family* and *food* are a good place to start. Word sleuths can then interview people in their communities, looking for translations of these words in a variety of languages. Establish a place in the classroom where students can mount a visible collection.

Our Words Tell Us Who We Are

English has borrowed from many languages:

algebra and *orange* from Arabic; *thug* from Hindi; *woodchuck*, *chili*, and *Mississippi* from Native American; *ski*, *sky*, and *steak* from Scandinavian. The *al* beginning of algebra is a clue to word sleuths that the word comes from the Arabic. *Al* is the Arabic definite article corresponding to *the* in English. *Alcohol* and *alkali* are also Arabic words. *El Niño*, the warming of the ocean surface off the western coast of South America, is derived from Spanish for the Christ child. In the nineteenth century, fishermen in Peru noticed that this phenomenon occurred around Christmas time and so named it. Bartolommeo Eustachi, a sixteenth-century Italian anatomist, described the tube that connects the middle ear cavity with the throat, but most people don't realize that their body part is an eponym. Word stories abound—as a character in Penelope Lively's *Moon Tiger* observes, "We open our mouths and out flow words whose ancestries we do not even know. We are walking lexicons. In a single sentence of idle chatter we preserve Latin, Anglo-Saxon, Norse: we carry a museum inside our heads, each day we commemorate peoples of whom we have never heard."

At the same time we are looking at the fascinating influences on English, we must not forget the distinctly American contributions. *America in So Many Words: Words That Have Shaped America* by David Barnhart and Allan Metcalf tells fascinating stories of significant words through the years. Starting with *turkey* in 1607 and progressing through *apple pie* in 1697, *banjo* in 1740, *cookbook* in 1809, *goober* in 1834, *bloomers* in 1851, *P.D.Q.* in 1875, *bulldozer* in 1930, *DJ* in 1950, and ending with *millennium bug* in 1998, the book offers words for every year, words that Americans have added to the English language and words that have particular meaning in our history.

Students will be interested to know that in 1618 *punk* was a kind of overcooked corn prepared by Indians in Virginia. By 1889, it was a slang term for a cigarette. During World War II, it referred to a small-time hoodlum. And these days, it's associated with rock music.

In the 1600s, when white settlers in North America saw an enormous, awesome animal, they borrowed a name from either Italian *bufalo* or Portuguese or Spanish *búfalo*. This word that has become so distinctly American might also be traced to the Greek *boubalos*, meaning an antelope or Old World mammal such as the water buffalo. *Bison* is the preferred term for the North American mammal but *buffalo* is older.

Buffalo has given its name to a major Great Lakes city in New York, as well as to some twenty other U.S. cities. A *buffalo wing* is a fried chicken wing served with hot sauce and blue cheese dressing. It gets its name from the New York city where it was first served. A *buffalo soldier* was a member of one of the African American regiments within the U.S. Army after the Civil War. The *American Heritage Dictionary* says this is a translation of a Kiowa term, from "the perceived similarity between the soldiers' hair and the hair on a buffalo's head."

There are other buffalo words, items that don't seem to have much to do with the awesome creatures of the plains. A *buffalo gnat* is a black fly, a *buffalo beetle* a carpet beetle, a *buffalo berry* a shrub. *Buffalo fish* are suckers found mainly in the Mississippi valley. There is also *buffalo clover, buffalo grass, buffalo plaid,* and *buffalo weed*.

Squaw is another word with a distinctly American history. Now listed as "offensive" or "highly offensive" by many dictionaries, it didn't start out that way. Linguists agree that it comes from the Algonquian *woman, young woman, queen,* or *lady*. No matter how it started, many Native Americans, particularly women, are insulted by its use today, saying that no matter how the word originated, current usage is always derogatory. They feel the U.S. Board on Geographic Names should order a blanket change of *squaw*, a name used in more than one thousand American place names. Others disagree, feeling affronted by the thought of changing the name of the town or mountain or river they have known for generations.

People can name man-made features such as streets, airports, or schools anything they want. But names of geographic features—the place names used on Federal documents such as topographic maps of the U.S. Geological Survey—must be approved by the U.S. Board on Geographic Names. And occasionally the board steps in and orders a change. In 1967, the board ordered a change of the 143 place names employing *nigger*, another word with straightforward beginnings that has taken on monumental negative baggage.

Some states are making the squaw name change on their own. For example, in 2000, Maine ordered the word erased from the map. *Big Squaw Township* became *Big Moose Township*, and thirty similar name changes resulted throughout the state. Five other states passed similar laws. In Montana, *Squaw Mountain* became *Dancing Lady Mountain*, and so on. The struggle has been fierce to change the name of Squaw Peak in Arizona; some have expressed doubt that Squaw Valley, a former Olympic site in California, will ever be changed.

Others disagree with these name changes. Marge Bruchac, an Abenaki woman, traditional storyteller, and historian, questions "the motion to gut our original language in the name of the political correctness." Bruchac says "We—Indian and non-Indian writers—are not yet of one mind, although at least we are communicating." Bruchac's views are available at: *www2.enia.net/users/dpanther/page10.html* and *http://freepages.genealogy.rootsweb.com/ ~ massasoit/bruchac.htm*

The point here is not to enlist students to rise up against the word *squaw*. The point is to help them understand and appreciate the power of words. A highly charged word like *squaw* gives importance to the study of other words. Consideration of squaw place names offers students a lesson in language use, history, government policy, social action, and most of all a lesson in the fact that words count, that words connect to community. In 1995, students at Cass Lake-Bena High School learned a lot about fund-raising as well as history and political activism when they successfully petitioned county commissioners to

Web Watch

The students' story is available at: *http://nativenet.uthscsa.edu/archive/nl/9610/0029.html*.

change the name of *Squaw Point*, on the Leech Lake Reservation in Minnesota, to *Oak Point*.

Although Chapter 3 focuses on names in a more playful way, the complications in the use of *squaw* as a place name are mentioned here both as a possibility for student investigation and as a reminder of Wendell Berry's injunction that we must stand by our words. To this end, it is both useful and necessary for students to learn that a word is more than its dictionary definition, and that words change. When students—even those pushed out of their high school right before the administration of a high-stakes test for their so-called "lack of interest"—are encouraged to explore language, anything can happen. For example, Steve Orel's students at the World of Opportunity in Birmingham, Alabama gave him a lesson in hip-hop, showing him a variety of ways to say *I've got to go.*" Cortney, Cedric, Alex, and John came up with these variations:

- I've got to dip.
- I've got to bounce.
- I've gotta jet.
- I've gotta catch a cut.
- "Holler"
- Bun-out!
- B-out.

Steve used this information to develop a lesson on standard English. The character in Penelope Lively's *Moon Tiger* didn't sit in on this lesson, but she summarizes its significance when she observes, "I never cease to wonder at it. That words are more durable than anything, that they blow with the wind, hibernate and reawaken, shelter parasitic on the most unlikely hosts, survive and survive and survive."

References

Adult Books

Allington, Richard. "Critical Balances: Early Instruction for Lifelong Reading." (*www.readingonline.org/critica/houston/alling.htm*).

Anderson, Richard C., Elfrieda H. Hiebert, et al. *Becoming a Nation of Readers: The Report of the Commission on Reading.* (Center for the Study of Reading 1985).

Barnhart, David and Allan Metcalf. *America in So Many Words: Words That Have Shaped America.* (Houghton Mifflin 1997).

Berry, Wendell. *Standing by Words.* (North Point Press 1983).

Blachowicz, Camille and Peter Fisher. *Teaching Vocabulary in All Classrooms.* (Prentice-Hall 1996).

Bruchac, Marge. "Thoughts on Indian Images, Names, and Respect." (*http://freepages.genealogy.rootsweb.com/~massasoit/bruchac.htm* 1999).

Bryson, Bill. *Made in America: An Informal History of the English Language of the United States.* (Morrow 1994).

———. *The Mother Tongue: English and How It Got That Way.* (Morrow 1990).

Burke, Jim. *The English Teacher's Companion.* (Boynton/Cook 1999).

Carey, Susan. "The Child as Word Learner" in *Linguistic Theory and Psychological Reality*, edited by M. Halle, et al. (MIT Press 1978).

Christenbury, Leila. *Making the Journey: Being and Becoming a Teacher of English Language Arts*, 2nd edition. (Boynton/Cook 2000).

Claiborne, Robert. *Our Marvelous Native Tongue.* (Times Books 1983).

Cunningham, Anne E. and Keith E. Stanovich. "What Reading Does for the Mind." *American Educator.* (American Federation of Teachers Spring/Summer 1998) (*www.aft.org/publications/american_educator/spring_sum98/cunningham.pdf*).

Cutler, Charles L. *O Brave New Words!: Native American Loanwords in Current English.* (University of Oklahoma Press 1994).

Farb, Peter. *Word Play: What Happens When People Talk.* (Knopf 1974, 1993).

Flexner, Stuart Berg. *I Hear America Talking.* (Touchstone 1979).

Foster, Don. *Author Unknown: On the Trail on Anonymous.* (Henry Holt 2000).

Garrison, Webb. *Why You Say It.* (MJF Books 1992).

Geller, Linda Gibson. *Word Play and Language Learning for Children.* (National Council of Teachers of English 1985).

Greenman, Robert. *Words That Make a Difference* (Levinger Press 2001)

Grimes, Barbara F. (ed.). *Ethnologue*, 13th edition. (Summer Institute of Linguistics 1996).

Harmon, Janis and Wanda Hedrich. "Zooming In and Zooming Out: Enhancing Vocabulary and Conceptual Learning in Social Studies." *The Reading Teacher* 54(2), 2000.

Heller, Louis G. and Alexander Humez and Malcah Dror. *The Private Lives of English Words.* (Wynwood Press 1984).

Hendrickson, Robert. *QPB Encyclopedia of Word and Phrase Origins.* (Facts on File 1997).

Illich, Ivan. *In the Vineyard of the Text.* (University of Chicago 1993).

Isil, Olivia A. *When a Loose Cannon Flogs a Dead Horse There's the Devil to Pay.* (International Marine 1996).

Krashen, Stephen D. *Every Person a Reader.* (Language Education Associates 1996).

———. *The Power of Reading: Insights from the Research.* (Libraries Unlimited 1993).

Lance, K. "The Impact of School Library Media Centers on Academic Achievement" in *School Library Media Annual* 12, edited by C. Kuhlthau, 1994.

Lively, Penelope. *Moon Tiger.* (Grove 1997).

McKean, Erin (ed.). *Verbatim: From the Bawdy to the Sublime, the Best Writing on Language for Word Lovers, Grammar Mavens, and Armchair Linguists.* (Harcourt 2001).

McQuillan, Jeff. *The Literacy Crisis: False Claims, Real Solutions.* (Heinemann 1998).

Meider, Wolfgang and Deborah Holmes. *Children and Proverbs Speak the Truth: Teaching Proverbial Wisdom to Fourth Graders.* (University of Vermont 2000).

Merriam-Webster. *The Merriam-Webster New Book of World Histories.* (Merriam-Webster 1991).

Metcalf, Allan. *The World in So Many Words.* (Houghton Mifflin 1999).

Nagy, William E. *Teaching Vocabulary to Improve Reading Comprehension.* (National Council of Teachers of English 1988).

Nagy, W., R. C. Anderson, and P. Herman. "Learning Word Meanings from Context During Normal Reading." *American Educational Research Journal* 24: 237–70, 1987.

Partridge, Eric. *Origins: The Encyclopedia of Words: Their Meanings, Etymology and Uses Through History.* (Macmillan 1959).

Room, Adrian. *Dictionary of Changes in Meaning.* (Routledge & Kegan Paul 1986).

Rosenbaum, Catherine. "A Word Map for Middle School: A Tool for Effective Vocabulary

Instruction." *Journal of Adolescent and Adult Literacy* 45(1): 44, 2001.

Smith, Frank. *The Book of Learning and Forgetting.* (Teachers College Press 1998).

Stahl, Steven. *Vocabulary Development.* (Brookline Books 1999).

Strauss, Valerie. "Educators Split on Whether Workbooks Work and Lists Lift Students' Word Knowledge." *The Washington Post,* September 11, 2001.

Wells, Diana. *100 Flowers and How They Got Their Names.* (Algonquin 1997).

———. *100 Birds and How They Got Their Names.* (Algonquin 2002)

Children's Books

Florian, Douglas. *Bing Bang Boing.* (Harcourt Brace 1994)

———. *Insectlopedia.* (Harcourt Brace 1998).

———. *In the Swim.* (Harcourt Brace 1997).

———. *Laugh-eteria.* (Harcourt Brace 1999).

———. *Lizards, Frogs, and Polliwogs.* (Harcourt Brace 2001).

Hepworth, Cathi. *Antics!* (Putnam 1992).

———. *Bug Off!* (Putnam 1998).

Milne, A. A. *Winnie the Pooh.* (Dutton 1926).

Most, Bernard. *There's an Ant in Anthony.* (Mulberry 1992).

Parish, Peggy. *Amelia Bedelia* series. (Multiple books, multiple publishers.)

Potter, Beatrix. *The Tale of the Flopsy Bunnies.* (Frederick Warne 1909).

———. *The Tale of Squirrel Nutkin.* (Frederick Warne 1903).

Wilbur, Richard. *The Pig in the Spigot.* (Harcourt 2000).

Yep, Laurence. *Later 'Gator.* (Hyperion 1995).

2

The Matter and Marvel of Dictionaries

"How many words are in the dictionary?" Eight-year-olds aren't the only ones asking this question. The question is the basis of sales campaigns for unabridged dictionaries, with competing publishers vying for the title of whose is bigger. But the answer depends on who's counting—and how they are counting. One way dictionary makers inflate their numbers is to include obscure variations of key words.

A more basic question might be "How many words exist?" Or, better yet, "How many words do we need?" According to the Wordman on yourdictionary.com, "As of 11:16 A.M. (Pacific) on June 29th of the year 2001, there were approximately 816,119 words in the English language, plus or minus a handful." The Wordman adds, "Choose well among them."

Choose well. The writers of the *King James Bible* used fewer than 20,000 different words. But what words they were, informing the style and vocabulary of works ranging from Negro spirituals to the Gettysburg address to scores of contemporary writers. William Shakespeare, ranking as one of the most famous and revered writer in the history of English literature, drew on 24,000 different words to complete his works.

Practically speaking, people call their dictionary "unabridged" if it contains somewhere between 400,000 to 600,000 words. That's quite a word explosion. If Shakespeare made do with 24,000, who's using the other 576,000? More than 40 percent of the entries in an unabridged dictionary such as the *Webster's Third New International Dictionary* are scientific and technical terms, and a lot of the entries are different forms of the same word. College dictionaries generally contain from 130,000 to 160,000 entries, still a hefty number.

Plenty of people believe a dictionary is for browsing. Oliver Wendell Holmes advises, "When I feel inclined to read poetry, I take down my dictionary. The poetry of words is quite as beautiful as that of sentences. The author may arrange the gems effectively, but their shape and luster have been given by the attrition of ages." Pulitzer Prize–winning novelist Carol Shields begins her writing day by picking up the dictionary. She reads a page at random—every word. She says this immerses her in language, a crucial start to her day.

A Brief History

The earliest known dictionaries were found in the library of the Assyrian king Ashurbanipal at Nineveh. The cuneiform

Student: Dictionary Savvy

Show your dictionary savvy. Answer these questions:

- Name three things you can use a dictionary for.
- How is a dictionary arranged, and why do you think it's arranged this way?
- If you had the job of making a shorter dictionary, what words would you leave out?
- If you had the job of adding a new dictionary feature, what would you add?

Student: Words of Advice

Here's the problem: With new words appearing all the time, dictionaries are getting too large. Dictionary makers have a difficult time getting all the new words in while keeping the old ones. Do you think dictionaries should include all words or should they go back to the old style of including just "hard" words? Write a letter of advice to a dictionary publisher.

writing on clay tablets dates from the Seventh Century B.C. In 1440 in Norfolk, England, Galfridus Grammaticus, a Dominican monk also known as Geoffrey the Grammarian, compiled the *Promporium Parvulorum Sive Clericorum* (Storehouse for Clerics/Scholars/Students). Considered the first English dictionary, the work listed Latin equivalents of 10,000 English words. In the 1600s the first dictionaries giving definitions of English words in English appeared. These books contained only "hard" words, words people didn't understand.

In 1755, after eight years of hard work, Samuel Johnson published his two-volume *A Dictionary of the English Language.* Wanting to show how words are used, Johnson drew on 160,000 quotations to clarify the definitions of the 40,000 words in his dictionary. The dictionary bore the strong stamp of Johnson's personality: If a quote didn't quite suit his purpose, he changed it; if he disliked the style of an author he was quoting, he rewrote the selection.

Certainly dictionaries are not so idiosyn-cratic these days, but still they are the products of human hands and minds. As Jonathon Green shows in his fascinating *Chasing the Sun: Dictionary Makers and the Dictionaries They Made,* there is no perfect dictionary uninfluenced by a lexicographer's beliefs, prejudices, ethnicity, gender, and personality.

How Is a Dictionary Made?

There are three ways to make a dictionary:

- Record the words you hear.
- Copy words from existing dictionaries.
- Read a lot.

Devise a system for recording and sorting the words you've read. These methods, of course, overlap. All lexicographers use earlier dictionaries as reference, but Samuel Johnson changed dictionary-making forever when he chose the third method—reading—as the core of his methodology. Johnson bought books by the ton and hired six people to help him read them. Everyone wrote down the sentence in

Give student teams a word to study for one week. When they encounter their word while reading they should write down the sentence in which it appears. At the end of the week they should sort their sentences into *meaning* piles and present their findings to the class. Some possible words: *take, set, do, run, go, add, begin, miss, feel, try, line.*

WordCentral.com offers a sample of what curious readers might uncover in such an investigation. *Run* can mean *cost* (as in *What did your new car run you?*). It can also mean *resort* (*She runs to her mother at every difficulty.*); *glide* (*The file drawers run on ball bearings.*); *smuggle* (*He ran moonshine during Prohibition.*); and *print* (*Every newspaper is running the story.*). Golfers, croquet players, stocking-wearers, musicians, equestrians, card players, biologists, gardeners, and fishermen all have their own applications for *run.* In fact, the entry in *Merriam-Webster's Collegiate Dictionary* runs to more than eighty senses.

The second edition OED's longest entry is for the verb *set*, which uses about 60,000 words to define more than 430 senses. Revisions and additions are currently underway for the verb *make*, which put it at more than 70,000 words of text.

which a chosen word appeared. These sentences were then available for Johnson to consult when he was trying to explain the meaning of a word. This language-in-use was the triumph of Johnson's dictionary. Using illustrative quotations, Johnson listed 134 uses of the verb *take.*

A century after Johnson's dictionary appeared, plans were launched for the "big dictionary." Simon Winchester describes the plan in *The Professor and the Madman*:

> While Johnson had presented a selection of the language—and an enormous selection at that . . . this new project would present *all of it:* every word, every nuance, every shading of meaning and spelling and pronunciation, every twist of etymology, every every possible illustrative citation from every English author.

It took Johnson and his team six years to create their impressive work. It took the *Oxford English Dictionary* (OED) team seventy years.

The OED staff was helped by 2,000 volunteer readers. The readers' job was twofold:

- ■ Read a lot and make word lists of all they read.
- ■ Look for certain words of interest to the dictionary team.

The methodology established for these readers is the same one used by lexicographers today. The target word is listed on the top left-hand side of a slip of paper. Below is the date, the title of the book or paper, and its volume and page number. Below this is a full sentence that illustrates the use of the target word. Volunteer readers for the *Oxford English Dictionary* sent in six million slips of paper with illustrative sentences.

This method is still alive. The current chief editor of the OED is looking for help with a new revision, due out by 2010:

Web Watch

On March 13, 2000, Sir James Murray's five-year-old great-great-great grandson became the first person to use *OED Online*. The next day it was made available to everyone else (for a fee) at *oed.com*. Facts, history, and a dictionary are available at this address for no charge. You can download Oxford English Dictionary News for July 1999 and learn the great lengths to which editors went to track down the origin of the word *nachos* (*http://oed.com/public/news/9907_2 .htm*). It's a fascinating story and helps children gain new respect for the amount of work that goes into a dictionary revision.

Student Job Application: Dictionary Editor

When James Murray was considered for appointment as editor, he was asked to submit his work on sample words. He chose *arrow, carouse, castle,* and *persuade*. Your challenge is to apply for a job as a dictionary editor. To demonstrate your talent for this position, you must choose one or two words and prepare dictionary-style entries, with illustrative sentences showing the words' various meanings.

Suggestion: Choose a word you really like or a word that's important in your life.

Reminder: Dictionary entries may be illustrated.

Student: A Room of Your Own

After James Murray received the appointment as editor of the *Oxford English Dictionary,* he built a corrugated iron shed on the grounds of the school where he taught. He called this shed, where he planned to do the dictionary work, the *Scriptorium.* Your first challenge is to figure out why Murray thought this was such a suitable name. Your second challenge is to invent a name for a special room you'd like to build to reflect one of your interests. Submit a design for this room.

I would like to invite readers to contribute to the development of the Dictionary by adding to our record of English throughout the world. Everyone can play a part in recording the history of the language and helping to enhance the Oxford English Dictionary.

People interested in submitting words for the new OED can find a form at *http://oed.com /public/readers/submitform.dtl.*

The *New York Times* calls the *Oxford English Dictionary* "the greatest work in dictionary making ever undertaken." Work on the OED started in 1857, with Scottish lexicographer Sir James Augustus Henry Murray becoming editor in 1879. His granddaughter, K. M. Elisabeth Murray, wrote a fascinating account of the making of the OED, *Caught in the Web of Words.* For a riveting account of madness, violence, weird learning, arcane obsessions, and the triumph of an idea, read *The Professor and the Madman* by Simon Winchester.

The OED second edition appeared in 1989. Its 21,730 pages take up 20 volumes and weigh 137.72 pounds. That's 59 million words, using up 6,243 pounds of ink to make the print run. There are 291,500 entries. Containing 2,436,600 quotations, its most frequently quoted work is the Bible, with Shakespeare being the most frequently quoted author with 33,300 quotations (1,600 of these come from *Hamlet*).

Web Watch

Another Oxford site (*www.askoxford.com*) contains a variety of interesting segments. There are lots of questions and answers about words, some history, some games. In Dictionary Questions, the Oxford Dictionary team answer questions people ask about dictionaries, including "Are dictionaries really necessary?" and "Do dictionary makers make mistakes?"

Teaching Tip

When selecting a children's dictionary, most teachers feel it is better that definitions list the current meaning first. Children learning to use the dictionary independently need the support of familiarity. Etymology and historical use are fascinating topics but generally require the assistance of an adult.

American Dictionaries

Noah Webster, famous for his *American Spelling Book* (1783), published *A Compendious Dictionary of the English Language* (1806). His major contribution to lexicography, *An American Dictionary of the English Language*, begun in 1807 and published in 1828, was notable for including typically American usage, as well as 12,000 more words and 40,000 more definitions than had ever appeared in any dictionary of the English language. The first Merriam-Webster dictionary was published in 1847. *Webster's Third New International Dictionary of the English Language*, published in 1961, created a furor with its inclusion of slang as part of its attempt to create a dictionary that reflected contemporary usage.

In 1894, Isaac Kauffman Funk came out with *A Standard Dictionary of the English Language*, introducing a new format for definitions. Funk began each definition with the current meaning of the word, listing older meanings in reverse historical order, followed by the etymology. Before Funk, dictionaries started with etymology and then traced historical uses. Funk's structure is strongly recommended for school dictionaries.

What Words Belong in the Dictionary?

The tremendous flap caused by *Webster's Third New International Dictionary of the English Language* was nothing new. When Samuel Johnson was getting ready to write his dictionary in the 1700s there was a lot of dis-

sension about what a dictionary should be. Many leading literary figures of the day thought the language needed to be *fixed*. They wanted to do what was already being done in France—create a national language standard, define and measure what is appropriate language. A national language authority would decide what could and could not be permitted. Jonathan Swift was one of the fiercest advocates of this view. He was outraged that words like *bamboozle* and *couldn't* were appearing in print. The author of *Gulliver's Travels* declared that the language needed rules. Swift and his group wanted a dictionary that would both define and maintain the purity of the language.

Samuel Johnson disagreed strongly, declaring in his dictionary's preface that it is not the lexicographer's task to "teach men how they should think, but relate how they have hitherto expressed their thoughts." Johnson actually started his dictionary with the intent of "fixing" English, but practicality soon demolished this intellectual theory. Johnson concluded that a dictionary can't "embalm" language or protect it from corruption any more than an elixir can guarantee eternal life. When praised by a woman for his restraint in leaving out "naughty" words, Johnson replied, "No, Madam, I hope I have not. . . . I find, however, that you have been looking for them."

Like the woman who praised Johnson's restraint for leaving out naughty words, children will search dictionaries for "those" words—and finding them creates a temporary stir. Don't worry about it. Who can trust a dictionary that carefully cuts all the emotionally charged vocabulary? Dictionaries don't titillate. They do, in fact, through their intellectualism, reduce the overblown impact of the kids' street knowledge of strong words. Finding a forbidden word in the dictionary can be the first step in understanding that it's "just a word."

When Sylvia asked me what a bastard was I took the class to the library to look up the word in the *American Heritage Dictionary*. A few teachers, scandalized by the dictionary,

Directions: Try to think of a word you predict won't be in the dictionary. Document your trials, giving a reason for your choices.

Proposed Word: _____

I predict it will be in the dictionary because _____

Is the word there? If so, what's the definition?

If the word isn't there, write a definition.

protested that such a book did not belong in a school library, giving students easy access to "those" words. As if our students aren't already surrounded by those words. None of the dictionary bowdlerizers seem to consider how young readers are supposed to have any respect for or interest in sanitized and circumscribed school dictionaries. Fortunately, our librarian, a wise and committed woman, one with boundless faith in children and in books, keeps the dictionary on the shelf. Years later as I loaded the CD-ROM of the *American Heritage Dictionary*, fourth edition, I was asked to choose between the version with or without "vulgar words." It feels odd for a teacher to choose vulgarity. If I'd written the installation instructions, I would have found a different way to put this.

Classroom Practice

Although the ability to use a dictionary is an important skill, assigning students the task of looking up and copying out definitions is not a recommended strategy for vocabulary growth. In short, it doesn't work. Unless and until students encounter words in meaningful contexts ten to fifteen times, they won't know the word. Copying a definition ten times is *not* "meaningful context." Dictionary definitions can help if a student already has some familiarity with the word, but as Stahl and Fairbanks report,

"just teaching definitions did not significantly affect children's reading comprehension." Definitions are important but not sufficient for understanding words. In *Words, Words, Words*, Professor Janet Allen titles a chapter "Alternatives to Look It Up in the Dictionary!"

Although skill-and-drill worksheets do not improve students' vocabulary comprehension, students do need to learn how to use dictionaries. They need to become adept at alphabetical order, using guide words, and learning to read the entries. The teaching goal must be to encourage student practice with using dictionaries and at the same time give them experiences that help them appreciate both the utility and the power of dictionaries.

Definition Game

Houghton Mifflin's Education Place runs *Fake Out!*, a game where children guess word definitions. Children are also invited to create fake definitions for specified words. They are also invited to guess which definitions are real and which are fake. For example, here's one *Fake Out!* entry; one definition comes from the *American Heritage Dictionary* and the rest are written by children (*www.eduplace.com/fakeout*):

The word *cilice* means:

- relating to a carrot
- a cake made from cider

- a citrus-flavored soda
- a key on a keyboard
- a device used for cooking
- a small piece of; a portion
- a truck-like vehicle used for transporting animals
- a coarse cloth
- a ceiling made of glass

Students don't need to rely on Houghton Mifflin. Encourage them to play classroom *Fake Out!* Point out that they need to read definitions in order to be able to write good ones.

Word Puzzlers

To teach something about word relationships while helping students gain ease in dictionary use, give students word families to explore. The Word Puzzlers on the next page help students get started on this concept. Note that a minimum is set (for example, find out what at least three have in common), leaving room for different students to consider varying amounts. Such puzzlers should be done over time, with plenty of discussion of each set of words.

Guide Words
Write a word on the board and challenge students to find it without opening their dictionaries more than four times. All of a sudden, guide words become very important.

One discussion starter is to ask students to brainstorm all the words they associate with the target word. Encourage them to make personal associations.

How Does a Word Get into the Dictionary?

Merriam-Webster OnLine: The Language Center says this is one of the questions most frequently asked of their editors. The short answer is, "People need to use it." The more complicated answer is that when a new word appears regularly in books, magazines, and newspapers, it becomes a candidate to enter the dictionary. To decide which words to

Word Fun

Find the Secret Word
Using this method, any student can locate any word in the dictionary someone has secretly chosen in fewer than fifteen guesses. But they have to follow the rules.

1. A Secret Keeper selects the secret word and writes it down, and gives it to the Witness.
2. The Guesser opens the dictionary to approximately the middle, asking, "Is it in this half?" It doesn't matter which half he chooses. Whether the Secret Keeper answers "yes" or "no," the Guesser now knows which half of the dictionary contains the word.
3. The Guesser now opens the half of the dictionary containing the secret word to the approximate middle, again asking, "Is it in this half?"
4. This method continues, with the Guesser dividing each section in half. He will soon be on the page containing the word. There, he asks if points to middle of page, asking, "Is it above this word?" And so on.

Students of all ages are crazy about this game. It reinforces alphabetization skills as well as encourages students to control their impulsiveness. Students quickly learn that wild guesses don't work. The game also inspires interest in words. The lowest number of guesses—seven—to locate the secret word was achieved by a group of high schoolers. Maybe your students can top it.

WARNING: Student enthusiasm with this activity takes a toll on dictionaries!

Word Puzzlers

Put these words in alphabetical order and find out what at least three have in common: diction, edict, contradict, dictation, dictionary, verdict, dictator, predict, indictment, interdict.

Put these words in alphabetical order and find out what at least three have in common: sympathy, synagogue, syndicate, synthetic, symbiosis, symmetry, symptom, symposium, synonym, photosynthesis.

Put these words in alphabetical order and find out what at least three have in common: grammar, autograph, epigraph, paragraph, graphology, autobiography, cardiogram, biography, orthography, graphics.

Put these words in alphabetical order and find out what at least three have in common: decalogue, pentagon, century, trilogy, trident, decapod, quadruped, octogenarian, centipede, quintuplet.

include in the dictionary and to determine what they mean, Merriam-Webster editors study the language to determine which words people use most often and how they use them.

Each day most Merriam-Webster editors read for an hour or two. They read books, newspapers, magazines, electronic publications. They call this activity "reading and marking" because they are looking for new words and new meanings of existing words. Editors explain, "Any word of interest is marked, along with surrounding context that offers insight into its form and use."

The marked passages are then input into a computer system and stored both in machine-readable form and on 3-by-5-inch slips of paper, called *citations*. Each citation has the following elements:

- the word itself
- an example of the word used in context
- bibliographic information about the source from which the word and example were taken

Merriam-Webster's citation files, which were begun in the 1880s, now contain nearly fifteen million examples of words used in context. A fifty-million-word database of citations is also available for dictionary editors to draw upon.

Before a new word can be added to the dictionary, the word must have enough citations to show that it is widely used. But if all of a word's citations come from highly specialized publications, the word might not make it into the dictionary because the citations reflect that it is the jargon of experts within a single field. In 1900, words were being added to dictionaries at the rate of one thousand a year. Now we add from fifteen thousand to twenty thousand new words a year. Many of these new words are scientific and technical words. When Random House produced the second edition of its twelve-pound unabridged dictionary, it included more than fifty thousand words that didn't exist twenty years earlier; it also had seventy-five thousand new definitions of old words.

Word Watch

As an Assistant Editor for the *Oxford English Dictionary*, Henry Bradley was in charge of the sections S–Sh, St, and W–We, among others. His treatment of *set* occupies twenty-three pages in the dictionary. Challenge students to see how many different uses of *set* they can come up with—before they look in a dictionary.

So dictionary editors have to figure out a way to make choices. Here's what they do at Merriam-Webster:

> To be included in a Merriam-Webster dictionary, a word must be used in a substantial number of citations that come from a wide range of publications over a considerable period of time. Specifically, the word must have enough citations to allow accurate judgments about its establishment, currency, and meaning.

But rules aren't enough. Dictionary editors have to exercise their own judgment. Sometimes a word is instantly important, as was the case in the 1980s with AIDS. Such a word goes into the dictionary even though its citations don't come from the number of years required of other entries.

The size and type of dictionary also affects how many citations a word needs to gain admission. Dictionary size is critical, and an abridged dictionary will contain only the most common words. Again, the Merriam-Webster editors explain, "a large unabridged dictionary, such as *Webster's Third New International Dictionary*, has room for many more words, so terms with fewer citations can still be included." Unabridged dictionaries also have room for other special features. *The American Heritage Dictionary of the English Language*, Fourth Edition, for example, touts its expanded word histories.

> In addition to etymologies, which necessarily contain information in a compressed form, this Dictionary provides Word History paragraphs at entries

A Word of Your Own

In *Frindle* by Andrew Clements, Nicholas Allen's fifth-grade teacher is a fanatic about the dictionary, which Nick finds to be a bore. Then Nick gets the big idea. He decides to create a word, and *frindle* is born. Nick and five friends sign a vow never to use the word *pen* again, using the word *frindle* instead.

Challenge: Invent a word.

1. Think about what kind of word you will create (noun, adjective, exclamation).

2. Invent your word.

3. Come up with a strategy to get your new word used widely.

Vowel or Consonant?

If your class were to write a dictionary, which letter would you want to be responsible for? Write a letter to the dictionary editor, explaining which letter you want—and why.

whose etymologies are of particular interest. In these Notes the bare facts of the etymology are expanded to give a fuller understanding of how important linguistic processes operate, how words move from one language to another, and how the history of an individual word can be related to historical and cultural developments. For example, the history of the word *alligator* involves borrowing from Spanish into English, as its etymology reveals, but the Word History also describes the role of taboo deformation in the history of the word *crocodile* and in that of *alligator* as well. Usually the Word History also contains the date at which the word was first recorded in English.

Specialized Dictionaries

Thesaurus

"The man is not wholly evil—he has a *Thesaurus* in his cabin."
—a description of Captain Hook
in *Peter Pan* by J. M. Barrie

In 1787, eight-year-old Peter Mark Roget started keeping a vocabulary notebook. He grouped words under headings such as *Beasts, Weather, People, In the Garden*, and *Different Things* in his notebook. Peter was a precocious student, entering Edinburgh University at age fourteen, graduating with an M.D. degree at age nineteen. Although he worked full time in medicine for the next twenty years, Peter didn't forget his interest in categorizing language. In 1805, Peter wrote an early draft of a book using the word system based on the categories he'd set up as a boy. This early manuscript contained fifteen thousand words, but for the next forty-seven years Peter kept it private, using it only as his own private treasure trove for his own writing, to help him convey precise meaning. After retiring from his post as secretary to the Royal Society, Peter turned to polishing his "thesaurus of English Words and Phrases," and at age seventy-three, he decided to publish it. Peter's son directed the

Word Watch

Ask students to consider why Roget's book is called a *thesaurus*, which comes from the Greek word for *treasury* or *storehouse*.

▌▏▌▏▌▏▌▏▌▊▏▌▊▏▌▊▏▌▊▏▊▏▊▏▊▏▊

publication in 1852, of the first edition of *Roget's Thesaurus*, containing 990 classes of words. When Peter died in 1869, the book had gone through twenty-four editions. It has never been out of print. The 1992 edition contains more than 250,000 words. Peter's system of classification is the same format used today with information retrieval in computer databases.

When *Roget's Thesaurus* editor Robert Chapman died at age eighty-one, the *New York Times* described him as an editor "who built a distinguished career on the difference between the right word and the almost right word." In preparing the fifth edition of Roget's book, Chapman resisted the pressure to list entries in alphabetical order, which many argued are more user-friendly. But Chapman did overhaul the subject headings to reflect modern concerns. Some of the thirty new categories he added include *Substance Abuse*, *Fitness*, *Exercise*, and *Computer Science*. With 1,141 pages, this fifth edition weighs four-and-a-half pounds. Chapman named his twenty-six-foot sailboat *Thesaurus*.

Teaching Tips

How do you encourage and inspire students to avoid overworking certain familiar words—*big, small, hard, easy*? Typical worksheets on using the thesaurus don't help because they encourage tedium, not thoughtfulness. Children will dutifully copy five words that mean *big*, but because this is a copying chore, they rarely remember the words once they've completed the chore. The following classroom-tested strategies inject some fun, creativity, and opportunity for oddball inventiveness into the exercise.

Creative Cartoons
Use an idea from an old *New Yorker* cartoon to help students expand their vocabularies. A large dinosaur is shown with a thought balloon containing the words *large, great, huge, considerable, bulky, voluminous, ample, massive, capacious, spacious, mighty, towering, monstrous*. The caption to the cartoon is *Roget's Brontosaurus*. Offer the idea to your budding cartoonists: What would the thought balloon for *Roget's Rattler* contain? *Roget's Turtle? Roget's Chimpanzee? Roget's Pest? Roget's Perfect Ice Cream Cone?* and so on. The possibilities are limitless.

Reading Connection
A Snake Is Totally Tail by Judi Barrett provides a good introduction to this exercise. Barrett notes distinctive characteristics for a giraffe who is *noticeably neck* and a skunk who is *oodles of odor,* among others. One caution: Point out to children that when trying to decide on animal characteristics for this exercise, some choices are "better" than others in that they invite more synonyms. *Red,* for example, has scores of variations, but *mouth* not as many.

Extensions
■ Invite students to choose two animals and use thought balloons to show how each animal sees the other.
■ Students can use this synonym balloon technique to illustrate a famous simile (or cliché): *wise as an owl, brave as a lion,* and so on. Students should list as many synonyms for the adjective as possible.
■ Challenge students to create an alphabetic list of animal characteristics.
■ If you're having a good classroom day, invite students to draw you, complete with your thought balloon. Inviting such whimsy and good-natured kidding is a super classroom technique.

Word Watch

A New Yorker on vacation wrote the *Metropolitan Diary* feature of the *New York Times* about a sign posted in the basement of the Berkshire Museum in Pittsfield, Massachusetts (the basement houses creatures like frogs, turtles, snakes, and a chameleon as well as the aquarium):

PLEASE DO NOT
Abuse, aggravate, agitate, alarm, anger, annoy, badger, beset, bother, bullyrag, disquiet, distress, disturb, exasperate, fluster, frighten, frustrate, goad, harass, harm, harry, hassle, heckle, hound, hurt, intimidate, irritate, jeer, maltreat, molest, nettle, persecute, perturb, pester, plague, provoke, rattle, ruffle, scare, shock, tantalize, tease, torment, torture, tousle, upset, vex, or worry THE ANIMALS.

Activity: Alert readers may notice that some letters aren't represented. Maybe they'd like to fill in with some words.

Alternative Activity: Challenge students to create an alphabetic list of ways to please people (and other animals). The directions in this case would be PLEASE DO.

Thesaurus with Something Extra

Random House Word Menu by Stephen Glazier is a word reference book organized by subject matter. So if one is looking for a kind of chair or sofa, one would find the general category *Home*, the subcategory of *Furnishings*, and then *Chairs and Sofas*, all sixty-five of them—a description of everything from Adirondack chair through butterfly chair, potty chair, settee, throne, and wing chair. Then you can move on to thirty-three types of beds. Under the general category of *Human Body*, subcategory *Medical Problems*, one finds 251 *Diseases and Infestations*. The book is a reverse dictionary, a glossary with eight hundred divisions, an almanac, and a thesaurus.

Rhyming Dictionary

There are, of course, rhyming dictionaries for adults. *Time to Rhyme: A Rhyming Dictionary*

Web Watch

At *www.Bartleby.com*, Peter Roget's classic structure is coupled with C.O. Sylvester Mawson's modernization, providing 85,000 hyperlinked cross-references. As an added bonus, 2,900 proverbs and quotations from classic and modern authors illustrate the thesaurus entries. Thesaurus.com also provides synonyms for words of your choice.

by Marvin Terban does the job for young readers. As Terban points out, "Only common one-syllable words are in this book." Terban makes the book easy to use and cautions students that words that rhyme might not have the same spelling at the end, for example, *bird, heard, herd, purred, stirred, word*. Every class needs a comprehensive rhyming dictionary. A good place to start is *Merriam-Webster's Rhyming Dictionary*.

Brewer's Dictionary of Phrase and Fable

This dictionary is a golden oldie, first published by the Reverend Ebenezer Cobham Brewer in 1870 and updated ever since. It is the source book for cultural references, where you can find the meaning of things you can't find in the dictionary or the encyclopedia—everything from *death from strange causes* to *naughty figs* to the *national anthem*. It is very handy to be able to look up these things online at the veritable bartleby.com, but when you have the book in front of you, one good thing always leads to another.

Another site, *www.bibliomania.com*, gives a more booklike experience. Choose the first letter of the item you want to look up and a group of expressions starting with that letter appears. Here's a sample:

Jack Robinson; Before you can say Jack Robinson Immediately. Grose says that the saying had its birth from a very volatile gentleman of that name, who used to pay flying visits to his neighbours, and was no sooner

RhymeZone (*www.rhymezone.com*) provides provocative online rhyming possibilities. Among other things, the site offers one hundred and thirty words and phrases that rhyme with *brick*. A nice feature of this site is that words are arranged by syllable. In the one-syllable category both words and nonwords are given, with the nonwords muted. Such lists provide a fun and instructive look at rhymes that extend beyond the one-syllable variety. Just seeing *frog kick, magic trick,* and *licorice stick* dramatically expands the 10-year-old poet's imaginative horizon.

1 syllable
bic, bick, blick, bric, bryk, chick, click, crick, cwik, dic, dick, dicke, dyk, dzik, fick, ficke, flick, frick, fricke, gick, glick, hick, kick, klick, knick, krick, kwik, lick, mic, mick, micke, nick, nik, pic, pick, pik, prick, quick, quik, ric, rick, ricke, schick, schlick, schmick, schnick, schrick, schtick, shick, shtick, sic, sick, slick, smick, spic, sprick, stick, strick, swick, thick, tic, tick, trick, vic, vick, vik, wick, wicke, wik, wyk, zick, zwick

2 syllables
afflik, be sick, card trick, cue stick, deer tick, fish stick, free kick, frog kick, handpick, hard tick, horse tick, house dick, ice pick, joss stick, mouse click, nonstick, oil slick, old nick, place kick, pool stick, salt lick, sheep tick, size stick, soft tick, sword stick, throw stick, vandyck, vanwyck, vanwyk, wood tick

3 syllables
carrot stick, control stick, corner kick, dolphin kick, double quick, flutter kick, hockey stick, magic trick, nic, pogo stick, polo stick, scissors kick, shooting stick, sleepy dick, swagger stick, swimming kick, throwing stick, trisomic, walking stick

4 syllables
celery stick, conjuring trick, licorice stick, measuring stick, ostpolitik, realpolitik, slippery dick

5 syllables
devil's walking stick

6 syllables
american dog tick

announced than he was off again; but the following couplet does not confirm this derivation: "A warke it ys as easie to be done / As tys to saye Jacke! robys on."

Jack Sprat A dwarf; as if sprats were dwarf mackerels. Children, by a similar metaphor, are called small fry.

Jack Tar A common sailor, whose hands and clothes are tarred by the ship tackling.

Jack and the Bean Stalk A nursery tale of German invention. The giant is All Father, whose three treasures are a harp (i.e., the wind); bags full of treasures (i.e., the rain); and the red hen that laid golden eggs (i.e., the genial sun). Man avails himself of these treasures and becomes rich.

Jack of All Trades In French, the saying is "Master of None": "Tout savoir est ne rien savoir."

Brewer's Dictionary of Phrase and Fable, Sixteenth Edition, revised by Adrian Room, contains one thousand new entries not available online (online versions are from the 1894 revision). Room's updated entries include *blockbuster, main squeeze, millennium bug,* and *Hulk, the Incredible.* Plenty of the entries are still obscure to most modern eyes: a list of the fifty Nereids listed in Edmund Spenser's *The Faerie Queen*, and the twelve oldest British public schools for girls, to name just two. But this in no way distracts from the pleasure this erudite (and somewhat dotty) volume gives. A reviewer called it "the world's best bathroom book"; it can also be a teacher's "best lunch break book." Browse here and you are sure to find lore to share with students.

Spelling Bee Words

The Scripps Howard Company, which sponsors the Scripps Howard National Spelling Bee, publishes *Paideia*, a booklet of words used in the spelling bee. More than three thousand seven hundred words are grouped into twenty-nine categories. The categories range from weather words to words found in the works of Edgar Allan Poe to words derived from Spanish to astronomical terms to words from entomology, plus lots more.

Scripps Howard also maintains a website with information and study tips about their spelling bee and about words in general: *www.spellingbee.com*. Each week *Carolyn's Corner* at the website discusses another category of words found in *Paideia*. *Rooting Around* provides an in-depth look at some feature of the words discussed in *Carolyn's Corner*, such as affixes or word origins.

Special Words

Homophones

Eight Ate: A Feast of Homonym Riddles and *The Dove Dove: Funny Homograph Riddles*, both by Marvin Terban, are two resources that demonstrate to children just how much fun words can be.

And why should kids have all the fun? *Homophones and Homographs: An American Dictionary* by James B. Hobbs is a fascinating read. On first glance, it might not seem likely that a dictionary of three thousand six hundred homophones and six hundred homographs would make for riveting reading but

this one is definitely more absorbing than one might anticipate. The author confesses that he got hooked on homophones as a result of school project of his friends' son in Allentown, Pennsylvania. With the help of family and friends, each second grader was to come up with a list of homophones, such as *dear* and *deer*. (Homographs are spelled the same but different in pronunciation and meaning, like *row* [to propel a boat] and *row* [a fight]).

Long after the second grader had finished his project, the author was still searching for homophones. He abandoned haphazard strategies for a "systematic cover-to-cover examination of two abridged dictionaries" and then two times he went through the 460,000 entries in the 2,710-page *Webster's Third New International Dictionary of the English Language*.

Here are a few samples—for grown-up *Amelia Bedelia* fans:

air: atmosphere
are: 100 square meters

Word Watch

Invite students to read an *Amelia Bedelia* book or two. Then challenge them to see who can collect the most homophones. The winner in the Allentown second grader's class amassed 356 words.

Word Watch

The word most often asked about at *http://dictionary.cambridge.org* in October, November, and December 2001 was *serendipity*. *Dictionary* was number five; *terrorism* and *anthrax* ranked ninth and tenth in queries.

The word *serendipity* was coined from the Persian fairy tale *The Three Princes of Serendip* in 1754. Invite students to coin a word from a fairy tale they know. For example, what might *goldyloxed* mean?

yourdictionary.com

This site has links to more than 2,000 dictionaries in more than 260 languages. Their specialty dictionaries include Cooking, Crafts, Humor, Medicine, Sports, plus eighty more. In the *Quick Lookup* section, a student can search for a definition from the dictionary or some synonyms from the thesaurus. The site contains a *Word of the Day*, with pronunciation, definition, usage, and etymology. One can sign up to have the daily word appear in a daily email message. There is also a *Spanish Word of the Day* and a *Chinese Word of the Day*.

There are word games for adults and children. And, courtesy of the University of Pennsylvania Museum of Archeology and Anthropology, students can find out how to write their names in ten languages, including Babylonian Cuneiform, Egyptian Hieroglyphs, Chinese, Eskimo, and Viking Runes.

www.bartleby.com

This site contains the *Columbia Encyclopedia, Sixth Edition, American Heritage Dictionary, Fourth Edition, Roget's II: The New Thesaurus, American Heritage Book of English Usage*, three books of famous quotations, *King James Bible, Oxford Shakespeare, Gray's Anatomy, The Harvard Classics and Shelf of Fiction, Strunk's Elements of Style, World Factbook*, and *Columbia Gazetteer*, Emily Post's *Etiquette*, Frazier's *Golden Bough*, Robert's *Rules of Order*, Mencken's *The American Language*, and *Fanny Farmer's Cookbook*.

This site also contains the published works of a limited number of authors. If you look up, say, Emily Dickinson, you get an essay about her life and work from the *Cambridge History of American Literature* as well as her complete poems. You also get a provocative quote from Emily:

My hair is bold like the chestnut burr; and my eyes, like the sherry on the glass that the guests leave.

www.worldwidewords.org

The subtitle of this site is "Investigating International English from a British Viewpoint." It is fun and illuminating for adults, and adults who find fun in words also find ways to transmit this fun to the children in their care.

http://www.m-w.com/dictionary.htm

This site is titled *Merriam-Webster OnLine: The Language Center*. In addition to dictionary and thesaurus "look it up" features, the site contains a Word of the Day (which you can get delivered to your email) and *Word Games*. It also provides access to *yourdictionary.com,* where you gain access to 1,800 dictionaries in 230 languages. The site has lots of other features—layers and layers for exploration. *Words from the Lighter Side* contains entertaining and informative excerpts from some Merriam-Webster books:

Flappers 2 Rappers: American Youth Slang, What's in a Name? Reflections of an Irrepressible Name Collector, Coined by Shakespeare: Words and Meanings First Used by the Bard.

The offerings in *Words from the Lighter Side* change each month—and there's an archive. *Cool Words* include such things as *Mess Hall Metaphor*, which discusses some of the slang used to describe military food during World War II. One can find the meaning and derivation of such terms as *battery acid, cow juice, goldfish, fish eyes, mystery, shingles.* Such words provide a fun opportunity for looking at metaphor.

The *Language Info Zone* contains articles about the history of English and other related topics. It also has selections from *The Barnhart Dictionary Companion*, a quarterly publication devoted to tracking changes in the English language and to documenting new words.

Word for the Wise archives are at this site. These daily two-minute radio programs aired on National Public Radio explore language, providing fascinating tidbits about words. Two years worth of scripts are available. Here's the scoop on *humble pie*:

Originally, that dish referred to a pie made of the umbles or edible viscera of a deer that was fed to servants after a hunt. These days, humble pie is more commonly used to name "a figurative serving of humiliation, usually in the form of a forced submission, apology, or retraction."

http://wordcentral.com

This site, operated by Merriam-Webster, is designed for children. It features a student dictionary as well as a variety of activities to engage children in word fun. Children can subscribe to *Daily Buzzword* and receive word info as email. *Build Your Own Dictionary* asks, "Have you discovered a great new word? Let the world know!" Students are invited to check words that have been submitted by others and to submit their own. For *discovered*, read *invented*. Although not stated, the implication is that these are invented words—in the tradition of Lewis Carrol and Dr. Seuss. The student contributions include: *gwiggle, numhand, ophiolium, shwash*, and *nastifying. Nastifying* is an adjective meaning "very gross or disgusting" and was invented in 2001.

In the *Computer Lab* students can type in a text and choose one of three encoding methods in which to encode their text. Here's what happens:

Text entered: Now is the time for all good people to come to the aid of the party.

Encoded in Secret Cipher: Abj vf gur gvzr sbe nyy tbbq crbcyr gb pbzr gb gur nvq bs gur cnegl.

There is also a *Verse Composer* feature. It is formulaic at the lowest level, but some students will have a good time, and others will figure out how to improve the formula.

e'er: contraction of ever
ere: before
err: make a mistake
eyre: journey
heir: inheritor

heroin: narcotic made from morphine
heroine: principal female character in
drama, novel, or event

maize: Indian corn
Mays: fifth month
maze: intricate passages

Like eating peanuts, it's hard to stop once
you start in this dictionary.

Capitonyms

A capitonym is a word that changes pro-
nounciation *and* meaning when it is capital-
ized. For example, *Job* is a character in the
Old Testament, but *job* is something we all
have to do. Here are a few more capitonyms
for students to figure out.

August	august
Polish	polish
Herb	herb
Rainier	rainier
Nice	nice
Tangier	tangier

The Matter and Marvel of Dictionaries

References

Adult Books

Allen, Janet. *Words, Words, Words.* (Stenhouse 1999).

American Heritage Dictionary, 4th edition, CD-ROM. (Houghton Mifflin 2000).

Brewer, Ebenezer Cobham. *Brewer's Dictionary of Phrase and Fable.* (Harper 1970).

Glazier, Stephen. *Random House Word Menu.* (Random House 1997).

Gove, Philip Babcock (ed.). *Webster's Third New International Dictionary.* (Merriam Co. 1976).

Green, Jonathon. *Chasing the Sun: Dictionary Makers and the Dictionaries They Made.* (Henry Holt 1996).

Hobbs, James B. *Homophones and Homographs: An American Dictionary.* (McFarland 1993).

Hopkin, Daniel J. (ed.). *Merriam-Webster's Geographical Dictionary.* (Merriam-Webster 1995).

Knowles, Elizabeth (ed.). *The Oxford Dictionary of New Words.* (Oxford 1998).

Landau, Sidney I. *Dictionaries: The Art and Craft of Lexicography.* (Cambridge 1996).

Mencken, H. L. *The American Language.* (Knopf 1962).

Morris, William. *The American Heritage Dictionary.* (Houghton Mifflin 1978).

Morton, Herbert C. *The Story of Webster's Third: Philip Gove's Controversial Dictionary and Its Critics.* (Cambridge 1994).

Murray, Elisabeth. *Caught in the Web of Words: James Murray and the O.E.D.* (Yale University 2001).

Oxford English Dictionary. *http://oed.com.*

Partridge, Eric. *A Dictionary of Slang and Unconventional Usage.* (Macmillan 1970).

Rodale, J. I. *The Synonym Finder.* (Rodale 1961).

6,000 Words: A Supplement to Webster's Third New International Dictionary. (Merriam 1976).

Stahl, S.A. and M.M. Fairbanks. "The Effects of Vocabulary Instruction: A Model-Based Analysis." *Review of Educational Research* 56: 72–110, 1986.

Unger, Harlow Giles. *Noah Webster: The Life and Times of an American Patriot.* (Wiley 1998).

Willinsky, John. *Empire of Words: The Reign of the OED.* (Princeton 1994).

Winchester, Simon. *The Professor and the Madman.* (HarperCollins 1998).

Children's Books

Amato, Mary. *The Word Eater.* (Holiday House 2000).

Barrett, Judith. *A Snake Is Totally Tail.* (Atheneum 1983).

Brooke, William J. *A Is for AARRGH!* (Joanna Cotler/HarperCollins 1999).

Clements, Andrew. *Frindle.* (Simon & Schuster 1996).

Terban, Marvin. *Eight Ate: A Feast of Homonym Riddles.* (Houghton Mifflin 1982).

———. *The Dove Dove: Funny Homograph Riddles.* (Clarion 1988).

———. *Time to Rhyme: A Rhyming Dictionary.* (Wordsong/Boyds Mills Press 1994).

3

Words Close Up and Memorable

Eponyms: What's in a Name?

Names are special. When students hear stories about how people, places, and objects got their names, they begin to look at words in new ways. Names are not accidental but the result of the way people see the world.

Take car names, for instance. In 1913, Henry Ford called his first car the Model-T. In 1956, when the Ford Motor Company introduced a revolutionary new automobile, it considered more than six thousand names before choosing one. Ford officials asked Marianne Moore, the distinguished poet, to invent a name for their new car. They told her they wanted a name that would give cus-tomers the idea of elegance and fleetness. Ms. Moore's suggestions included the Ford Silver Sword, the Pastelogram, Mangoose Civique, Anticipator, Intelligent Whale, and the Utopian Turtle Top.

Ford officials rejected Ms. Moore's suggestions. After consulting marketing research experts and looking at thousands of other names, including Zip and Drof (Ford spelled backward), Henry Ford named the car for his late son, Edsel. Three years after launching the famous car, the Ford Motor Company announced the end of production of the Edsel, and the name *Edsel* entered the language as a synonym for *dud*.

Other cars named for people have been more successful. Antoine de la Mothe Cadillac, who landed at Fort-Pontchartrain-du-Detroit on July 24, 1701, is considered the founder of Detroit. The luxury car bearing his name has been a symbol of prestige for many decades. The German luxury car Mercedes Benz was named for Mercedes, the daughter of one of the company executives.

Cars whose names come from people introduce students to the fascinating topic of eponyms. Searching the world for other eponyms shows students that word study can be fun as well as informative.

Web Watch

- This site provides a list of Japanese car names: *www.crossroads.net/h1/nihonsha.html.*
- Here are two sites on the origin of car names: *www.cybersteering.com/trimain/history/names.html* and *www.users.wineasy.se/elias/bilnamn.html.*
- A letter writer to "Cartalk" muses about car names that don't mean anything: *http://cartalk.cars.com/Mail/Letters/2000/05.19/3.html.*

■ Invite students to provide convincing arguments about whether Marianne Moore's suggestions would or would not make good car names.

■ Ask students to examine the connotative qualities of, for example, *Intelligent Whale*. How does calling a car a whale differ from calling it a mustang, a lynx, or a turtle?

■ Students can make a chart, dividing the animal kingdom into "good" and "bad" names for cars.

■ Should word choices be different for motorcycles? Tractors? Bicycles? Motorboats? Airplanes? Why or why not?

■ Challenge students to invent a musical instrument that uses their name. After studying music reviews in magazines and/or newspapers, they should write a review for a recital that features a solo piece performed on their namesake.

■ Ask students to invent a piece of clothing that derives from their name. They should name it and create either a catalog description or a newspaper or TV ad for this clothing.

■ Car buffs can look at the names of contemporary cars and conduct research to find out how one got its name. Ask literary sleuths to find out if car names today are different from names forty or fifty years ago.

■ History buffs can research the significance of the names of famous ships, buildings, and wars. For example, how did the Battle of Jenkins' Ear get its name?

■ Ask students to make an argument for a clothing "look" featured by someone today that may be an eponym ten years from now. **Tip:** Students often confuse brand names such as Calvin Klein with eponyms such as Stetson. "Jordans" may become an eponym; the Gap won't—unless they invent a unique piece of clothing.

■ Invite students to investigate some of these scientific eponyms: watt, volt, Celsius, curie, Fahrenheit, baud, ampere, Beaufort scale, Richter scale, Bunsen burner, diesel, Geiger counter. For students of more militaristic bent, there's bowie knife, guillotine, Molotov cocktail, shrapnel.

Eponyms Are for Wearing

From Levis to leotards, eponyms are popular garb. Bloomers, Stetsons, mackintoshes, and Wellingtons all have their own stories. Alert students will notice that you can eat one type of Wellington and wear another, both named for the same British general and statesman. The raglan sleeve is also named for a British military man, as is the cardigan sweater.

The jacket known as the sherwani in India is known as the Nehru in the United States, named for India's first prime minister, Jawaharlal Nehru.

Toot Your Own Eponym

Antoine Joseph Sax invented the saxophone, the only reed instrument made entirely of metal. The instrument became immediately popular after Sax first played it in Paris in 1844. An accomplished musician, John Philip Sousa joined the Marine Band at age thirteen. He is better known for the composition of more than one hundred marches, which earned him the title "March King." Sousa invented the eponymous sousaphone, a large, circular tuba.

Other Amazing Eponyms

In his introduction to *Let a Simile Be Your Umbrella*, William Safire tells a charming story about having lunch with Frederic Cassidy, editor of the famed *Dictionary of American Regional English* (DARE). The waiter asked, "Would you like a Bibb lettuce salad?" The great lexicographer looked off into the distance and said, "I wonder who Bibb was." Then they discussed the possibilities through lunch. As it turns out, Bibb was Major John Bibb, a leading amateur horticulturist of the nineteenth century who developed a form of lettuce in the greenhouse behind his Kentucky home. Bibb never sold the lettuce but gave it and the seeds to friends and neighbors who called it "Mr. Bibb's lettuce." These days, when new foods are called things like "hybrid 1530," it's nice to think of a lettuce named for someone of generous spirit.

The majestic evergreen trees found in

Read More

Guppies in Tuxedoes: Funny Eponyms by Marvin Terban.

A Chartreuse Leotard in a Magenta Limousine by Lynda Graham-Barber.

The Name's Familiar: Mr. Leotard, Barbie, and Chef Boyardee by Laura Lee.

The Name's Familiar II by Laura Lee.

Naming New York: Manhattan Places and How They Got Their Names by Sanna Feirstein is written for adults but is fascinating for readers of all ages. You don't have to be from New York to be fascinated to learn why places are named what they are.

California are named for Sequoya, the Cherokee leader who developed a syllabary for the Cherokee language. His system spread and by the 1840s two newspapers were published in Cherokee. Other popular flower and plant names come from Michel Begon, a seventeenth-century French patron of science; Louis Antoine de Bougainville, an eighteenth-century French navigator; George Joseph Kamel, a seventeenth-century Moravian Jesuit missionary; Anders Dahl, eighteenth-century Swedish botanist; William Forsyth, an eighteenth-century British botanist; Friedrich Heinrich Theodor Freese, a nineteenth-century German physician; Leonard Fuchs, a sixteenth-century botanist and physician; Alexander Garden, an eighteenth-century Scottish-American botanist; James Harvey Logan, a nineteenth-century American lawyer; Joel Roberts Poinsett, ninteenth-century American diplomat; Olof Rudbeck, seventeenth-century Swedish botanist. Renown botanist Thomas Nuttall, whose firsthand knowledge of North American flora was unmatched, named *wisteria*

Web Watch

The Chrysler car history site (*www.chrysler.com /inside/heritage/index.html*), searchable by decade, includes names.

What's Really in a Name?

Sometimes we get so used to car names that we don't think about what they really mean. Look at the Name column for actual cars and think about what the word means. Then write or draw about the name's possibilities on the road. The samples will help you get started.

Make	Name	Comment
Daihatsu	Charade	Is this an object pretending to be a car?
Honda	Acty Crawler	What happens when you get on the freeway?
Ford	Crown Victoria	
Mitsubishi	Mirage	
Dodge	Neon	
AMC	Gremlin	
Toyota	Stout	
Dodge	Viper	
Plymouth	Barracuda	
Subaru	Justy	
Suzuki	Esteem	
Ford	ZX2	

Now it's your turn! Find some car names you think are and are not appropriate.

Make	Name	Comment

floribunda for Dr. Caspar Wistar, eighteenth/nineteenth-century American anatomist who was an enthusiastic botanist as well as a friend of Thomas Jefferson. Nuttall got the spelling wrong. He realized his mistake but his attempts to correct the spelling of wisteria were unsuccessful. Nuttall, an Englishman, spent thirty years exploring the flora and fauna of North America. The pica nuttalli, the yellow-billed magpie, is named for him, as is the common poorwill, the Phalaenoptilus nuttalli (*Phalaenoptilus* meaning *moth-feathered*). Nuttall also had a woodpecker named for him.

Toponyms: Another Name for It

Toponyms are like eponyms except their names come from places rather than people. Denim, for example, comes to us from Nimes, France, manufacturing site of the popular cloth. People shortened *serge de Nimes* (cloth from Nimes) to *denim* (de Nimes). Duffel bags are named for a fabric made in Duffel, Belgium. The name for the bikini comes from a small island in the Pacific ocean. The Charleston, a popular dance of the 1920s flapper era, got its name from Charleston, South Carolina, which, in turn, got its name in 1620 from King Charles II. The Lindy Hop originated in Harlem and celebrated Lindbergh's solo flight across the Atlantic, so it would have to be the Harlem Hop to be a toponym. Another dance, the tarantella, got its name from Taranto, Italy. The Afghan hound's name comes from Afghanistan, as does the knitted blanket of the same name. The canary got its name from the Canary Islands in the Atlantic ocean off Africa. These islands got their name because they were overrun with dogs and the Latin word for dog is *canis* (*Canaria Insula*, "Isle of Dogs"). The bayonet, originally a short dagger, takes its name from Bayonne, France, where it was first made in the seventeenth century.

Eponyms Are for Eating

Eponyms usually pay tribute to people who invent something, but food eponyms are different, sometimes honoring the person who creates a new culinary delight or someone he admires; other times the food eponym honors the person who first eats it. *Caesar salad*, for example, is named for Caesar Cardini, who owned a restaurant in Tijuana, Mexico, called Caesar's Place. According to eponym lore, he invented this salad for Hollywood stars who crossed the border to eat at his restaurant in the 1920s.

Peach melba is named for Helen Porter Mitchell Armstrong, who left her husband and child in Australia and moved to England

Word Watch

Inventing Eponyms

- Student teams can create a menu for eponymous foods using their names. They can name the foods and describe them, including illustrations.
- Students might also search for eponymous food names at local restaurants.
- Thinking of how *Armstrong* became *Melba*, students can try creating new surnames from places they've seen—or been—or would like to visit.

▮▮▮▮▮▮▮▮▮▮▮▮▮▮▮▮▮▮▮▮

Word Watch

Investigating Eponyms

It's a Fact: Apples Charlotte are named for a character in a wildly popular novel by Johann Wolfgang von Goethe.

- Invite students to invent a food for a literary character.

It's a Fact: Napoleons are named for Napoleon, the famous French military commander and emperor. Napoleon is said to have eaten chicken flavored with tomatoes, onion, mushrooms, garlic, and olives to celebrate his victory over the Austrians at the Italian village of Marengo. Today we call this dish *Chicken Marengo*. *Beef Wellington* is named for the British commander who defeated Napoleon at Waterloo.

- Invite students to create a dish for a famous person in history. For example: What might a Lincoln be? A Truman? A Frederick Douglass?
- Invite students to create a food specialty named for a place they've been, or a place they'd like to visit.

▮▮▮▮▮▮▮▮▮▮▮▮▮▮▮▮▮▮▮▮

A World of Names

Directions

Toponyms are things whose name comes from a place in the world. Your task is to find some toponyms in the world around you and put them on the map.

First, choose a category: *birds and animals, food,* or *clothing.* For example, if you choose birds and animals, you will discover that *canary* gets its name from the Canary Islands and *afghan dogs* from Afghanistan. Where will you put Clydesdales? The Saint Bernard? If you choose to investigate food, where will you put *bologna*? If you choose clothing, where will you put *jeans* and *dungarees*?

For an eponym feast, students can go to *www .spellingbee.com/feast.htm*. Students participating in the Scripps-Howard National Spelling Bee contributed more eponyms at *www.spellingbee.com /cc02/Week04/eponyms.htm*.

to become an opera singer. She changed her name to Nellie Melba, because the surname reminded her of her home city of Melbourne. Nellie became so famous that a London chef named melba toast in her honor, and Escoffier, the famed chef at the Savoy Hotel, created peche melba, a dessert of peaches and vanilla ice cream in her honor. Eggs Benedict was named for someone named Benedict, but whether it was Samuel, Lemuel, or LeGrand depends on which story you believe. In any case, the dish was created for a customer named Benedict at a Manhattan restaurant, some say Delmonico's, others the Waldorf Hotel. Nobody remembers the name of the chef—just the man who ate the eggs. In 1876, a chef at Delmonico's created baked Alaska—in honor of the newly purchased Alaskan territory.

More Eponyms and Toponyms and How They Got That Way

J. Lechmere Guppy, the president of the Scientific Association of Trinidad, Venezuela, discovered a small fish that is native to the area around Trinidad, presenting this fish to the British Museum. The scientific name for this tropical fish is *Poecilis reticulate*, but everybody calls it the *guppy*.

William Russell Frisbee founded the Frisbee Pie Company in Bridgeport, Connecticut. In the 1920s, once students at Yale University had eaten the pie they threw the tin around. In the 1950s, the Wham-O Toy Company tried to market a flying saucer toy called the Pluto Platter, but when the executive heard about the game they played at Yale, he changed the name.

Students who collect fabulous words for the fun of it are well on their way to vocabulary expertise. These words may be challenging, amazing, weird, or just plain fun. Learning about food eponyms is a good enticement for starting a word collection about eating. Here are a few from *Playing with Words* by Margie Golick. This list lets students know that not only can they collect nice words; they can also invent some.

Crunchy, munchy, chewy, slurpy
Dippy, flippy, frosty, freezy
Fishy, squishy, squashy, squeezy
Juicy, bitey, bubbly, burpy
Mashy, splashy, floaty, fluffy

And then there's Alexandre-Gustave Eiffel, France's master of metal. Nicknamed Madicien du Fer, or the Iron Magician, Eiffel's name graces the famous tower he designed.

Some other fascinating origins include surgical gauze, also known as cheesecloth, which takes its name from the place it was first made, Gaza, Palestine. Venetian blinds weren't invented in Venice, but the people in the Italian city are the ones to popularize this Persian invention. Capitol, one of those words causing confusion, has ancient origins. Congress meets in the Capitol Building on Capitol Hill (*capitol* comes from the Capitoline Hill, the highest place in ancient Rome), but Washington, D.C., is the capital of the United States.

Some people think the Baby Ruth candy bar is named for the baseball star, but actually it was named in honor of Ruth Cleveland,

Read More

Invite students to check the library for a book about things named for real people. Laura Lee has written two informative and entertaining titles, *The Name's Familiar: Mr. Leotard, Barbie, and Chef Boyardee* and *The Name's Familiar II*.

Put Your Name in the Headlines

Think About It

Do you want your name to go down in history for finding a fish, inventing a game, designing a building . . . or something else? Once you decide, write the newspaper story announcing the feat. Here are some headlines to help you get started. (Note that Sara named the planet for herself.)

EXTRA! EXTRA!

Saraphus: New Planet Discovered by 10-year-old!

BUSINESS NEWS

The Candyman Corporation Announces New Confectionary: *Heavenly Bob*

Directions

Your turn—create newspaper headlines out of these suggestions.

The Nebraskan, a new _____

sensation, _____

Deep Sea Divers Discover (make up the name of a sea creature, using part of your

name or a friend's name), a _____

Architects Complete Construction of the _____,

a _____

Now that you've warmed up, create an object, name it, and write a news story about it.

the infant daughter of President Grover Cleveland.

Over six billion Oreos are sold annually, but there's no "Mrs. Oreo." The fig newton isn't named for Isaac, but Milton Hershey gave his name to the candy bar as well as well as to the town in Pennsylvania that houses the largest chocolate factory in the world. Orville Redenbacher decided his name on a line of popcorn would sell better than calling it Purdue-20 or Hybrid Dent. Harry Heinz's company was actually producing sixty-five products when he named he came up with the slogan *57 varieties*, but Harry liked the way *57* looked in print.

Sir Hugh Beaver, managing director at the Guinness Brewery, was out hunting and wondered if the golden plover was the fastest bird in the world. This gave him the idea for a book which informed the reader of the fastest, slowest, oldest, youngest, and so forth. He looked around for writers and found Norris and Ross McWhirter, identical twins who had a passion for collecting odd bits of information. The first *Guinness Book of Records* appeared in 1955, and was an immediate bestseller.

Numerous flowers are named in honor of the Virgin Mary, including marigold, Mary lily, rosemary, and lady's slipper. The lady bug also gets its name from this same source. Sometimes a plant's name depends on its national heritage. Both the English and the Scots acknowledge a flower named for William, Duke of Cumberland, who defeated the Scots in the Battle of Culloden in 1746. The English call the flower *sweet William* and the Scots *stinky billy*.

We have borrowed a lot of terms from heroes of Greek mythology. Atlas, one of the Titans, was forced by Zeus to hold up the heavens, an image that later changed to Atlas holding up the ball of earth. Gerhard Mercator, sixteenth-century Flemish geographer, included this image of Atlas on the title page of his collection of maps, calling the collection an atlas. A famous and ill-fated luxury liner also took its name from the Titans.

Word Watch

Challenge students to look on their supermarket shelves for products that might be eponyms or toponyms. They should write down the name of the product and check the label for the name and address of the manufacturer. Then they can write the company, asking how the product got its name. The Internet is another source for product information, though students should be cautioned that just because they read something there does not mean it's accurate.

▪▪▪▪▪▪▪▪▪▪▪▪▪▪▪▪▪▪▪▪

Many American place names derive from Native American words. Take Yeehaw Junction, Florida. *Yeehaw* isn't a hillbilly term but comes from *yaha*, the Seminole word for *wolf*.

A number of people are named for states, but the story of Virginia Hamilton's name tells a history of bravery. Ms. Hamilton came from a family of storytellers. Her grandfather Levi Perry was born a slave in Virginia and crossed the Ohio River to freedom. Once a year, Ms. Hamilton wrote, he gathered his children around him. "Sit down," he would say, "and I will tell you about slavery and why I ran, so that it will never happen to you." Ms. Hamilton was named Virginia in remembrance of his flight.

Place Name Panache
Place names is another area where our "borrowings" are visible. Different languages predominate in different areas of the country. For example, note the Spanish borrowings in the South and Southwest, the French in Louisiana, German in Pennsylvania and many Northern cities. The German-American bilingual communities in Chicago, Minneapolis, St. Louis, Milwaukee, and Cincinnati brought thousands of German words into American English.

In *Naming New York*, Sanna Feirstein provides an entertaining, historical account of how Manhattan's streets, squares, and neighborhoods came to be named, and in so doing shows how name research is history at its best. The famous Broadway was originally an Indian trail that ran from the southern tip of the island. Its name is literal, deriving from its unusual width. Harlem was named by the Dutch for the Haarlem they had left in Europe. The Bowery ran through an area set aside by early Dutch inhabitants for farming, "bowerji" being the Dutch word for farm. The British anglicized some Dutch names, so that the street named for Dirck Van der Clyff became Cliff Street, Markveldt became Marketfield, and so on. And Manhattan names keep evolving. SoHo, an acronym for South of Houston (Street), was adopted in the 1960s. TriBeCa, a named adopted in the mid-1970s, is an acronym for the TRIangle BElow CAnal Street.

In *Made in America*, Bill Bryson points out that until 1916, New Hampshire had a stream called the *Quohquinapassakessa-managnog*, but then some "cheerless bureaucrats at the Board on Geographic Names in Washington, D.C., arbitrarily changed it to *Beaver Creek*." The present-day *Connecticut* is the result of a number of name changes—Quonectacut, Quonaughticut, Qunnihticut, Conecticot, and so on. Bryson notes that "probably the liveliest diversity of spelling belongs to Chicago, which in its early days was rendered as Schuerkaigo, Psceschaggo, Shikkago, Tsckakko, Ztschaggo, Shecago, Shakakko, Stkachango,

Web Watch

Much of the contents of *What's in a Name* are available at the Merriam-Webster website (*www.m-w.com/lighter/name/aptronym.htm*); it's well worth a visit.

and many others, all trying to capture a certain sound."

The variety is fun, but the real point is the influence of Native American words on our landscape:

■ thirteen of the nineteen largest U.S. rivers (Mississippi, Ohio, Yuon, Missouri, Tennessee, Mobile, Atchafalaya, Stikine, Susitna, Arkansas, Tanana, Susquehanna, and Willamette);

■ ten of the major U.S. lakes (Michigan, Erie, Ontario, Okeechobee, Winnebago, Tahoe, Upper Klamath, Utah, Tustumena, and Winnibigoshish);

■ numerous natural wonders (Niagara and Yosemite; Denali, Sequoia, and Shenandoah national parks).

■ only two states of original thirteen colonies bear Indian names, but two-thirds of the last thirty-six do.

Word Watch

Students can begin an aptronym hunt with just a few categories and a supply of old telephone books. Ask student teams to scan pages for names that would be apt for doctors, lawyers, teachers, and people who work in restaurants. Each team can draw a letter out of a hat. Establish a grid on the bulletin board, where students can put in names as they find them. As one category fills, add others. As they come across provocative names, student teams are likely to want to add categories. This is a project some students enjoy working on independently. They may want to illustrate their work.

DOCTORS	POLICEMAN	TEACHERS	RESTAURANTEURS
Tom Coffin	James Copper	Andy Lerner	Alice Cook
Mary Cutter	Kevin Crook	Jane Crammer	David Cheeseman

Read More

Charles Cutler, author of *O Brave New Words! Native American Loanwords in Current English*, observes that Native American loanwords in English "are freighted with implied significance" and display an esthetic appeal beyond their intended use. In concluding his work, Cutler expresses the hope that greater awareness of these words will heighten our awareness of the Native Americans' lasting cultural impact in other ways.

More About Names: Aptronyms

Franklin P. Adams, a popular New York columnist and one of the original members of the Algonquin Round Table, coined the term *aptronym* to designate a name that is aptly suited to its owner.

According to a story in the *Washington Post*, when Pentagon reporters ventured north to Alaska, "the Northern Warfare Training Center assigned Lieutenant Colonel Will B. Snow to issue their Arctic gear." Snow's name is an aptronym lover's delight. Students will enjoy coming up with other suitable occupations for Mr. Snow.

Ask students to consider other people whose names match their occupations. Sally Ride, for example, is an astronaut. Students can consider other apt professions for someone with the last name of Ride. What would be another "apt" name for an astronaut?

Here are a few more aptronyms: John Buckmaster is a banker in Maryland; Linda Toot plays the flute in an orchestra in Florida; the Bury Funeral Home is in Buffalo; Gary Player is a professional golfer.

How People Get Their Names and How They Feel About It

From Rumpelstiltskin to Chrysanthemum, names are important in children's literature. Often characters have strong feelings about their names. Here are some provocative "name" snippets from popular tales that can act as conversations starters and as prompts for lots of possibilities.

> "Galadriel Hopkins. What a beautiful name! From Tolkien, of course."
>
> "No," muttered Gilly. "Hollywood Gardens."
>
> Miss Harris laughed a sort of golden laugh. "No, I mean your name—Galadriel. It's the name of a great queen in a book by a man named Tolkien. But you knew that."
>
> Hell. No one had ever told her that her name came from a book. Should she pretend she knew all about it or play dumb?
> —From *The Great Gilly Hopkins* by Katherine Paterson

> I have always hated my name: Enid Irene Crowley. Now really. It would be a terrible name even for an old women; for a fourteen-year-old girl it was unbearable.
> —From *Taking Care of Terrific* by Lois Lowry

> "Now, Miss Brownmiller," said the principal, "There must be a story behind your name as well. Don't tell me you're a witch."
>
> Salem laid her pencil down. "That's not far off, actually. My mother and father met each other in Salem, Massachusetts. My father says she

Teaching Tips

■ Ask students what image they get of the characters simply from their attitudes about their names. Which character would they like to know more about?

■ Invite students to contribute other name stories from books they are reading. They can create a "Name" bulletin board.

■ Invite students to write a letter of advice to one of the characters.

Fun with Aptronyms

Directions

Using names from your community, find an apt name for each occupation below. The newspaper or phone book is a good source for names. If you find other names that seem well-suited to particular occupations, add them to the list. The names around the border, taken from a phone book, will help you get started. You will see they are only from the beginning of the alphabet.

doctor	barber
grocer	botanist
truck driver	mathematician
lawyer	optometrist
baseball player	plumber

Find "apt" occupations for these people

Joe Bunt	Louis Chase
Art DeWire	Bill Dollar
Dorothy Reading	Tom Stamper
Juan Trippe	Bernard Twigg
Robert Furlong	Barbara Boxer
James Bugg	Dan Druff
John Lawless	Alex Hogg
Roger Roper	Chip Wood

bewitched him. He said he wanted his firstborn to be named Salem, whether it was a boy or girl."
—From *Report to the Principal's Office* by Jerry Spinelli

His grandmother had said that in the old days, people had a secret name that was known only to one other person—a name that described who they really were, not who the world thought they were. He had thought he would like to have such a name for himself, but this naming was no longer done. "I'll take a name for myself," he thought, eyeing the stone in his hand. "I don't need a father; I don't need any-one." Then he said aloud, "My name is Lone Bear."
—From *Bearstone* by Will Hobbs

Last year when David Bernstein was in third grade, there had been three other boys named David in his class. . . . David Bernstein did not like that a bit. It was much too confusing. Then, one day when he was reading a book called *The Arabian Nights*, he discovered a wonderful name: Ali Baba. There were no other Ali Babas in this class. And as far as David Bernstein knew, there were no other Ali Babas in his school. It was the perfect new name for a boy who wanted to be different.
—From *Hurray for Ali Baba Bernstein* by Johanna Hurwitz

Interesting and Unusual Names
In Julius Lester's *Sam and the Tigers: A New Telling of Little Black Sambo*, everybody has the same name:

> There was a little boy in Sam-sam-sa-mara named Sam. Sam's mama was also named Sam. So was Sam's daddy. In fact, all the little boys and little girls and mamas and daddies were named Sam. But nobody ever got confused about which Sam was which, and that's why nobody was named Joleen or Natisha or Willie.

Most people live in places quite different from Sam-sam-sa-mara and the choice of names—for children and pets and house-plants—is not automatic or prescribed. Some people want to name their children "regular" names so they won't be teased in school, so

Word Watch

In many Native American groups the name given to the male child must be one not currently in use by someone else. John E. Koontz at the University of Colorado, maintains a website where he answers lots of questions about Native American language. On his name page he says that "traditionally a man might run through several names in the course of a life . . . often trading up as a name with more panache became available." Parents sometimes changed a child's name to confuse evil influences or to mark a rite of passage.

Web Watch

Check out John Koontz's site: *http://spotcolorado .edu/~koontz/faq/names.htm*. Ask students if they could change their name as a rite of passage, say, when they become teenagers, would they do it? Why or why not?

Read More

Newbery Medalist Linda Sue Park's *When My Name Was Keoko* is inspired by the author's family stories of living in South Korea during the Japanese occupation before World War II. Japanese occupation forces required all Koreans to take Japanese names, which meant Sun-hee became Keoko, and she had to call all her classmates by their new names. This compelling story of two siblings and their battle to maintain their identity and dignity makes for a com-pelling read-aloud. As an interesting histori-cal note, Park reveals a little-known Olympic story about names. Kitei Son, wearing the Japanese flag on his shirt, won the marathon in the 1936 Berlin Olympics, the only time Japan has ever won the marathon. But Kitei Son was a Korean runner forced to run under an imposed name and flag; his real name was Sohn Kee Chung.

How Did I Get My Name?

Directions

Even if you think you know the answers to these questions, just to make sure, interview an adult in your family for help in answering at least two of these questions. You may uncover some interesting information about a very important person—you!

1. Who named me?

2. Was I named for anyone?

3. Why was this name chosen?

4. What does my name mean?

5. My nickname is . . .

6. I got my nickname when . . .

Choosing a Name

Read about the feelings of a boy who feels his parents made a mistake when naming him:

> Call me Bernie. All truly famous people need only one name. Like Superman and Bozo . . . What were my parents thinking when they picked out that name [Bernard]? They should have waited and asked me my choice. I'd have chosen an astronaut's name. Like Bim or Buzz or Gordo. Bernard is a name for a nerd, not an astronaut.
> —From *Bernie Entertaining* by Larry Bograd

■ Write a letter of advice to Bernie/Bernard.
■ Then write a letter of advice to new parents. What tips can you give them on naming the baby? Give examples to support your advice. For example, should names be popular? Or unique?
■ You may want to do some research on names. The Social Security Administration provides a website with the most popular given names in the US since 1880, *www.ssa.gov/OACT/NOTES/note139/note139.html*. Or just go to the Social Security page and enter "popular names" in Search.

TOP TEN NAMES FOR 2000

1. Michael	Hannah
2. Jacob	Emily
3. Matthew	Madison
4. Joseph	Elizabeth
5. Christopher	Alexis
6. Nicholas	Sarah
7. Andrew	Taylor
8. William	Lauren
9. Joshua	Jessica
10. Daniel	Ashley

TOP TEN NAMES FOR 1880

1. John	Mary
2. William	Anna
3. Charles	Elizabeth
4. George	Margaret
5. James	Minnie
6. Joseph	Emma
7. Frank	Martha
8. Henry	Alice
9. Thomas	Marie
10. Harry	Annie/Sarah (tie)

adults won't say, "Where did you get *that* name?" Other people prefer family names, names with special meaning, or out-of-the-ordinary names. Some people name their children for cities and states, such as Dakota, Madison, Trenton, and Savannah, to name just a few. Foreign place names are also popular, such as Paris, India, Martinique, and Persia.

The Place Names reproducible (see next page) is first for the fun of the sound of the words and then for thinking about. After students have tried out the alphabetic list of place names on their tongues, ask them to think about the names as possibilities for personal names. They can read the list independently or in groups and think about which ones they might choose for a name—and why. Ask students to consider how they make their choices; they should list some criteria.

Color Names

Colors provide more possibilities for naming. Paula Danziger's *Amber Brown* series has given fame to that word. There are lots more possibilities: Burgundy, Cerise, Ebony, Forrest, Grey, Hazel, Ivory, Jonquil, Kelly, Lilac, Mauve,

Place Names

Directions
Read this list of place names. Think about the way they sound and the way they look.

Aberdeen	Java	Reykjavik
Abilene	Jericho	Rio
Alaska	Jersey	Roanoke
Arizona	Jilin	Sacramento
Aspen	Jonquiere	Seychelles
Baja	Kagera	Shawnee
Brazil	Kahoolawe	Sicily
Brooklyn	Kentucky	Sydney
Burlington	Kenya	Tabora
Calcutta	Killarney	Tahoe
Calgary	Lamia	Tasmania
Cambria	Lammermoor	Tibet
Casablanca	Laramie	Ubangi
Cordova	Limoges	Udine
Dallas	London	Ukraine
Des Moines	Madrid	Umbria
Dijibouti	Maine	Umtata
Dominica	Milan	Venice
Eleuthera	Miami	Venta
Encinitas	Montana	Ventura
Erie	Narobi	Verseille
Euphrates	Navarre	Vienna
Everest	Nevada	Wembley
Falaise	Nigeria	Wenatchee
Famagusta	Nova Scotia	Wessex
Florence	Oberammergau	Wichita
Fremont	Oita	Windermere
Fresno	Oklahoma	Xanthus
Gambia	Oregon	Xenia
Gascony	Orissa	Xiamen
Geneva	Padua	Xingu
Ghent	Panaji	Xinjiang
Gisborne	Panama	Yalta
Halmahera	Pasadena	Yampa
Hama	Peleliu	Yao
Hastings	Qena	Yazoo
Hong Kong	Qishon	York
Ichikawa	Queens	Zambia
Ife	Quemoy	Zamora
Illinois	Quincy	Zermatt
Ireland	Raleigh	Zibo
Izmir	Rangoon	Zimbabwi

Color List

BLUE	PURPLE	RED	GREEN
baby blue	lavender	scarlet	emerald
azure	magenta	cherry	verdant
aquamarine	orchid	coral	olive
indigo	indigo	blood	pea
turquoise	mauve	lobster	jade
marine	violet	ruby	sea green
cobalt	hyacinth	brick	apple green
peacock	lilac	rosy	celery
robins-egg	mulberry	pink	parsley
lapis lazuli	burgundy	cardinal	chartreuse
periwinkle	periwinkle	strawberry	viridian
wisteria	plum	terra cotta	Nile
midnight	damson	Chinese	shamrock
Mediterranean	fuchsia	vermillion	hunter
teal	indigo	barn	Kelly
delphinium	heliotrope	fire	British racing
sapphire	maroon	crimson	jungle
cadet	hot pink	poppy	pistachio
Wedgewood	violet-red	salmon	khaki
navy	blue-violet	chestnut	lime
slate	amethyst	orange-red	forest

Color Choices

Directions

Share the color word list with a friend. Take turns reading the colors to each other.

1. Three names I like best are:

2. Three names my friend likes are:

3. We think these three colors are exciting:

4. Write ads to sell three items—a bicycle, a piece of clothing, or anything else you can think of. Be sure to mention the color of the item.

Color Mystery

The color list will be useful in completing this activity.

1. If you were writing a mystery in which someone had stolen a valuable antique vase,

   ▪ what color *blue* would you make it?

   ▪ what color *green* would you make it?

   ▪ Would you make the vase *banana yellow?* Why or why not?

2. List three things that might be called *banana yellow.*

3. If the hero or heroine of your story had *green* eyes, which green would you use?

4. What color would his or her hair be?

5. Try writing a parody of a heroic description, using any colors you wish. For example, it is one thing to say a woman's teeth are as white as ivory or pearls. It is quite another thing to say her teeth are as white as cottage cheese or Elmer's glue or boiled fish eyes.

Read More

For adult reading, there's *The Primary Colors* by Alexander Theroux—his three essays devoted to the colors red, blue, and yellow include every color allusion imaginable: artistic, literary, linguistic, botanical, cinematic, scientific, culinary, climatologial, and lots more. John Updike says Theroux has squeezed the world into this book. Here's a sample: Theroux points out that these things are yellow: the sun, cowardice, third prize, honey, school buses, urine, New Mexico license plates, Penzzoil, Easter, butter, arsenic, and Busby Berkeley's great banana epic starring Carmen Miranda, among others. Theroux also includes impressive trivia; he tells us that "a yellow baseball was actually used for the first time in the Major Leagues on August 2, 1938" (and he tells us the score of the game). And that an umbrella of yellow silk, a symbol of dignity, is one of the traditional Tibetan good-luck symbols. The sequel, *The Secondary Colors*, devotes 108 pages to orange, plus hundreds more to purple and green. There's also poetry, song, fable, opinion, gossip, and more fascinating trivia.

Ochre, Primrose, Russet, Saffron, Taupe, Umber, Virdinian, Yellow, and others.

- Make a Color Wall and students will come up with lots of variations on the theme.
- Ask students to keep track of color words they find in their reading. Not just the word but the sentence or paragraph in which it appears.

Names to Eat

Third graders collected ice cream names. Each time a student came in with a new name, he wrote it on a piece of adding machine tape strung down the hallway. To add a new name, students first had to read all the existing ones. No repeats allowed. This was not a chore but a popular pastime. Following are the names they collected; you may want to share this list with your students, but it would be more fun for them to collect their own.

lemon
vanilla
vanilla/chocolate
butterscotch swirl
chocolate swirl
cherry vanilla
Columbian coffee
chocolate chip
chocolate marshmallow
chocolate
French vanilla
cream 'n coffee fudge
black raspberry
vanilla/chocolate/butter pecan
mocha chocolate chip
black sweet cherry
mint chocolate chip
butter pecan

Student: Ice Cream Interview

Choose an ice cream poem or memory to share with at least two adults. First read the piece. Then ask the adults about their ice cream thoughts.

- You might ask about the adult's favorite flavor.
- You might ask for an ice cream memory.
- You might ask about something else.

At the end of the interview, ask the adult to give you two words about ice cream.

Ice Cream Poem

ice cream
ice cream
ice cream

You
I
We all
for
bites of
licking
delicious
tasting
remembering
chocolate
maple walnut
rocky road

scream
scream
scream
cold
ice cream
dripping
scrumptious
melting
flavors
strawberry
rum raisin
lemon

vanilla butter pecan
pistachio black sweet cherry
peanut butter cup
caramel apple dapple
bubble gum
black raspberry
coffee
coconut fudge
peppermint

licking
scooping up
sticky
melting
swirling
biting
slurpy
chewing
syrupy
hurry
ice cream
hurry
lick
chew
finish
before
dissolves
integrates
mantles
appears
appoints
a hole

licking
drops
sweet
licking
melting
silent
bites
sweet
urgency
before
puddles
scurry
quick
goo
goodness
cone
dis-
dis-
dis-
dis-
gets

and   happiness
drips drips drips drips drips drips
down   between   your
  sticky   fingers   drip
    drip   drip   drip
        drip   drip
            gone

Directions

Here's an ice cream poem written using ice cream words. Read them out loud with a buddy reader. Then collect your own ice cream words and write a poem.

© 2002 by Susan Ohanian from *The Great Word Catalogue: FUNdamental Activities for Building Vocabulary*. Portsmouth, NH: Heinemann.

strawberry
maple walnut
choclate buttered almond
rocky road
peanut butter cup
strawberry cheesecake
caramel apple dapple
cocoanut fudge
peaches 'n cream
rum raisin
peppermint candy

This list then became the word bank for lots of delicious short pieces of writing, mostly silly but sometimes reflective. From this initial list, we wrote ice cream poems; we wrote ice cream tongue twisters, riddles, menus, and memoirs.

When students write, I write too. That's the rule, and it gives an added incentive to make assignments interesting and inventive. On the previous page is an ice cream poem I wrote for a homework assignment. Students read it, filled in the blank spaces with ice cream names and sensations I'd left out, and they wrote their own ice cream pieces. You can guess what prefix we were studying at the time.

Here's another one I wrote just to hear the kids go "Ycch!"

VEGETABLE ICE CREAM

Many people dream
Of strawberry ice cream;
Chocolate's bite
Fills thousands with delight.
But me?
I long for a scoop of frozen pea,
Olive, mushroom, or Harvard Beet,
Carrot with sprinkles—now there's a
    treat
That can't be beat.
I would kick up a fuss for a three-decker
    cone of asparagus.
Vanilla does many please,
But can it compete with cheddar cheese,
Green pepper, broccoli, tomato, or yam?
Vegetable ice cream! Gee whiz! Wham!

Cold Words

When I began teaching at the junior high, I wondered if I could transfer the adding machine tape strategy. When one teaches students identified as high risk, one doesn't want to expose them to ridicule. I had certain doubts about seventh and eighth graders building up enthusiasm for displaying winter words on adding machine tape stretched down the hallway: But the dull, bare walls in our school were such a challenge. I found it a shame and an affront that student work was not on display in our school. And the adding machine tape device provides visible evidence that vocabulary is growing, not to mention that it provokes repeated reading from kids who carry a sophisticated repertoire of strategies for avoiding reading. So I took the risk. The rule here was the same as with the third graders: You have to read all the words before you can post a new word—no duplicates allowed.

The unexpected bonus of this activity was that it transformed my students into fervent newspaper browsers. I can't think of a better way to teach scanning skills. Students raced to class—to be sure to get hold of one of the five copies we received every day. Kids who read the paper at home thought they were pulling a fast one. Imagine a "reluctant reader" sneaking a read of the morning paper before heading off to school.

Here is a partial list of the words that stretched down the hallway of our junior high: Snow, slush, storm, icicle, blizzards, floods, freezing, frozen, chillier and chillier, Arctic air mass, shattered water pipes, hoarfrost, cold front, frigid, windchill factor, frostbite, North Pole, bitter cold, snowed-in, icy winds, ice, snowbank, shovel, snowball, whiteout, howling winds, rain, snow squalls, Brrr!, skiing, cold wave, hazardous driving conditions, freezing point, goose bumps, ZERO, frozen feet, polar bear, nippy, snowplow, swirling snowstorms, winter misery, deep freeze, blowing snow, shivering, blue with cold, Jack Frost, coldsnap, glacial, record-breaking cold, record cold paralyzes U.S.

Students engaged in fierce debates over the last two. Was the last one a repeat or not? Finally, "paralyzes" won the day and the phrase was admitted.

One of the benefits of this activity was students argued passionately over whether words qualified for the list. Determination to win an argument inspired lots of dictionary work. With word work, one thing leads to another, and *coldsnap* provoked interesting discussion about *cold-blooded, cold-hearted, cold-water flat, coldcock,* and *coldshoulder.*

Two weeks into the project, students began complaining bitterly when local journalists didn't come up with any new ways to describe our frigid weather. They'd rush in, grab the papers, read intently for five minutes and then sneer in disgust, "Same old words!" They began scanning my copy of the *New York Times* to see if out-of-town writers were doing any better. Michael commented, "We should be grateful we don't live in Florida" and then added, "Can you get us an Alaska newspaper, Miz O?"

The list became a word bank for the writing of winter memoirs and tall tales. But the best part of the project was the interest it generated throughout our eighteen-hundred-student school. There's something about a list that proves irresistible and students and faculty began stopping by each day to look for additions. Imagine how my students felt when they saw throngs outside our class reading *their* words. The certified rotten readers of the junior high were catapulted into the linguistic limelight—school experts on winter words.

American Names: A Rich Variety

Robert Louis Stevenson took a trip across the United States by train, remarking, "There is no part of the world where nomenclature is so rich, poetical, humorous, and picturesque as in the United States of America." Walt Whitman loved place names too. "Mississippi!" he exclaimed, "the word winds with chutes—it rolls a stream three thousand miles long . . . Monongahela!"

Teaching Tips

Point out to students that there are certain conventions to animal naming. Some people follow these conventions, other people don't. Name collector extraordinaire Paul Dickson points out that zoo animals get their names for various reasons. The famous pandas Ling-Ling and Hsing-Hsing were given names from their country of origin. Zoo llamas are often given names like Llulu. Here are some zoo gorilla names: Ramar, Sampson, Tanga, Shamba, Maximo, Massa, Kumba, Togo, Kanda. Dickson tells this story about how a gorilla at the Ringling Brothers–Barnum & Bailey Circus got its name. In 1937, the circus gorilla was named Buddy but the staff wanted something to convey its large size. They found a giant named Gargantua in a novel by Rabelais, and renamed Buddy Gargantua the Great. The adjective *gargantuan* has been popular ever since.

Some students like the idea of awful names. When asked the worst name for a horse he had ever heard, famed trainer Woody Stephens said, "Bug Juice." This is a story that grabs the attention of a twelve-year-old, but third graders like it too.

In his volume *The American Language* (available online at *www.bartleby.com*), H. L. Mencken said, "Some of the most mellifluous of American place-names are in the areas once held by the Spaniards. It would be hard to match the beauty of *Santa Margarita, San Anselmo, Alamogordo, Terra Amarilla, Sabinoso, Las Palomas, Ensenada, Nogales, San Patricio,* and *Bernalillo.*"

The Forty-Niners in the California Gold Rush weren't so melodious in their place naming, but they certainly were colorful: Jackassville, Whiskey Flat, Humbug City, Dirty Sock Hot Springs, Poker Flat, Muletown. Some claim the town of Paradise was actually named for the Pair o' Dice Saloon.

Frank K. Gallant, author of *A Place Called Peculiar: Stories About Unusual American Place-Names*, says as a ten-year-old he tried to get hold of Wilmer Mizell's baseball card because he loved the pitcher's nickname,

Naming Pets

In *The Very Kind Rich Lady and Her One Hundred Dogs* by Chinlun Lee, a very kind rich lady does have one hundred dogs, and she gives them all names.

■ Read the names out loud with a buddy reader and circle the ones you like best.

Papa	Pizza	Esme	Brutus
Mr. Samuel	Madeleine	Molly	Denver
Mary	Candy	Nova	Spider
Mrs. Fifi	Nero	Scamp	Sausage
Eeny	Pipi	Buster	Princess
Meeny	Nana	Billy	Curry
Miney	Flint	Toast	Charlotte
Mo	Mrs. Chips	Floss	Smoky
Sooty	Ruthie	Morris	Silk
Willow	Tuesday	Foxy	Ruby
Coco	Ginger	Peanut	Dizzy
Muffin	Abdul	Crispin	Harvey
Wesley J.	Pooch	Jasmine	Hobo
Camel	Jacket	Jumbo	Taffy
Yogurt	Tinkle	Tara	Mountain
Pudding	Tammy	Scat	Captain
Lola	Biscuit	Juno	Heidi
Lady	Toot	Wags	Hank Daisy
Honey	Crystal	Yum-Yum	Freddy
Queenie	Poppy	Pig	Groucho
Max	Arthur	Zaba	Harpo
Pepper	Tangle	Archie	Chico
Pirate	Fluff	Rusty	Mr. Scratch
Olive	Pretzel	Moff	Bingo
Julio	Henry	Darling	

■ Interview three people about how they chose a name for a pet. If you have a pet, you can interview yourself too.
■ Using information from the interviews, write an essay about how pets get their names.

Challenge: Can you come up with 101 good names for pets? Prove it!

Names of Virtues

Children born during Colonial times were often given the names of virtues. Some of these names are again popular. Read this list and see how many you know.

THE NAMES

Admiration
Adoration
Amity
Amnesty
Bliss
Bronchial
Benevolence
Charity
Chastity
Chivalry
Comfort
Constance
Courage
Delight
Dependability
Dignity
Elation
Emancipation
Endurance
Euphony
Faith
Fidelity
Freedom
Grace
Gumption

Halcyon
Harmony
Honor
Hope
Hosanna
Imagination
Innocence
Jocund
Joy
Keenness
Kindness
Liberty
Loyalty
Memory
Mirth
Modesty
Narcissus
Nobility
Obligation
Observant
Pacific
Panache
Patience
Peace
Prosperity

Prudence
Quietude
Radiance
Rejoice
Reliance
Remembrance
Resolve
Reverence
Sanctity
Serenity
Silence
Solace
Solemnity
Solidarity
Tolerance
Tranquility
Truth
Unity
Valor
Verity
Wisdom
Warmth
Watchful
Zeal

■ Choose at least ten words from this list to study. Write a letter of advice to parents explaining why one or more of the names would be an excellent choice for their child.

■ **Note:** There are two trick words on this list, two words probably nobody would want to be named. See if you can find them!

■ Come up with a name of opposite concepts, names that would be unfair to give a child (names such as Apathy, Cowardice, and Envy).

"Vinegar Bend," the name of the Alabama town where he was born. Frank admired his sister's boyfriend for making up stories about how the nearby Massachusetts towns got their names: Duxbury had to do with burying ducks; Sandwich was so named because that's what the first settlers ate at every meal. Despite his love for the imaginary, Frank grew up to travel around the country collecting the real stories of how towns got their weird names. "Why would someone name a town Toast? Intercourse? Santa Claus? Rough and Ready? Clever? Neversink? What was behind the name Peculiar, a perfectly ordinary Middle American town a short drive from Kansas City?"

From Eclectic, Alabama to Adamant, Vermont, town names can be quite a vocabulary excursion:

> Oracle, Arizona
> Paradox, Colorado
> Enigma, Georgia
> Aroma, Indiana
> Amity, Maine
> Gratitude, Maryland
> Nirvana, Michigan
> Novelty, Missouri
> Quietus, Montana (near Hanging
>   Woman Creek)
> Alliance, Nebraska
> Paradox, New York
> Chagrin Falls, Ohio
> Sublimity, Oregon
> Frugality, Pennsylvania
> Prudence, Rhode Island

There is a good story behind every one of these names. And if you look at them again, you'll see that each is a word likely to appear on the SATs or other standardized tests. Kids will love to know that Ambia, Texas is the only place in the world named for spit. According to Gallant, "The word was derived from the *amber* jets of tobacco juice expectorated by the men who congregated at the local store every afternoon to swap lies."

Word Watch

Garrison's Keillor's *Prairie Home Companion* acknowledges Georgia as a state with names like poetry: Mystic, Dewy Rose, Coofee, Ogeechee, Chicamauga, Chickaswatchee, Cisco, Oconee. Keillor notes that in Georgia you'll find Jerusalem, Jordan, Delhi, Damascus, Waterloo, Scotland, Vienna, Dublin, Macedonia, and Montezuma. Encourage students to find far-off place names in their own state.

▐ ▐ ▐ ▐ ▐ ▐ ▐ ■ ▐ ▐ ▐ ■ ▐ ■ ■ ■ ▐ ■ ■

Vocabulary lessons are all around us. Frank Gallant provides the weird ones. The classic compendium of all American place names is by George R. Stewart, *American Place-Names.*

Name That Storm: Tropical Cyclone Names

Hurricane is the name given to tropical cyclones that originate over the oceans. They were formerly identified by their longitude and latitude coordinates but authorities decided that short, distinctive given names makes for quicker, more accurate reporting. When there is more than one hurricane at a time, the use of distinctive names is important, helping to prevent confusion about what storm is moving where. Since 1953, Atlantic tropical storms have been named from lists developed by the National Hurricane Center and now maintained by an international committee of the World Meteorological Center.

Web Watch

- ■ The variety of worldwide cyclone names is fascinating; check them out at *www.nbc.noaa.gov /aboutnames.html.*
- ■ A clear, kid-friendly site with informative and appealing hurricane lore can be found at *www .usatoday.com/weather/whretire.htm.*

▏ ▏ ▎ ▋ ▏ ▋ ▏ ▎ ▏ ▋ ▎ ■ ▋ ▎ ■ ▎ ■

A storm is named when it reaches winds of 39 miles per hour. A storm becomes a hurricane when it reaches wind speeds of 75 miles per hour.

Until 1979, only women's names were used to designate hurricanes. Since then, men and women's names are alternated. Six lists are rotated. This means that in 2007, the 2001 list will be used again. If a storm is particularly deadly or costly, the name is not used again. Here are the Atlantic names.

2001	2002	2003	2004	2005	2006
Allison	Arthur	Ana	Alex	Arlene	Alberto
Barry	Bertha	Bill	Bonnie	Bret	Beryl
Chantal	Cristobal	Claudette	Charley	Cindy	Chris
Dean	Dolly	Danny	Danielle	Dennis	Debby
Erin	Edouard	Erika	Earl	Emily	Ernesto
Felix	Fay	Fabian	Frances	Franklin	Florence
Gabrielle	Gustav	Grace	Gaston	Gert	Gordon
Humberto	Hanna	Henri	Hermine	Harvey	Helene
Iris	Isidore	Isabel	Ivan	Irene	Isaac
Jerry	Josephine	Juan	Jeanne	Jose	Joyce
Karen	Kyle	Kate	Karl	Katrina	Kirk
Lorenzo	Lili	Larry	Lisa	Lee	Leslie
Michelle	Marco	Mindy	Matthew	Maria	Michael
Noel	Nana	Nicholas	Nicole	Nate	Nadine
Olga	Omar	Odette	Otto	Ophelia	Oscar
Pablo	Paloma	Peter	Paula	Philippe	Patty
Rebekah	Rene	Rose	Richard	Rita	Rafael
Sebastien	Sally	Sam	Shary	Stan	Sandy
Tanya	Teddy	Teresa	Tomas	Tammy	Tony
Van	Vicky	Victor	Virginie	Vince	Valerie
Wendy	Wilfred	Wanda	Walter	Wilma	William

References

Adult Books

Bryson, Bill. *Made in America*. (Morrow 1994).

———. *Mother Tongue: English and How It Got That Way*. (Morrow 1990).

Cutler, Charles. *O Brave New Words! Native American Loanwords in Current English*. (University of Oklahoma Press 1994).

Dickson, Paul. *Dickson's Word Treasury*. (Wiley 1982).

———. *Names*. (Delacorte 1986).

———. *What's in a Name? Reflections of an Irrepressible Name Collector*. (Merriam-Webster 1966).

———. *Words*. (Delacorte 1982).

Dunkling, Leslie. *The Guinness Book of Names*, 7th edition. (Facts on File 1995).

Feirstein, Sanna. *Naming New York: Manhattan Places and How They Got Their Names*. (New York University Press 2001).

Gallant, Frank K. *A Place Called Peculiar: Stories About Unusual American Place-Names*. (Merriam-Webster 1998).

Golick, Margie. *Playing with Words*. (Heinemann 1988).

Hamblyn, Richard. *The Invention of Clouds: How an Amateur Meteorologist Forged the Language of the Skies*. (Farrar, Straus, and Giroux 2001).

Harder, Kelsie B. (ed.). *Illustrated Dictionary of Place Names: United States and Canada*. (Van Nostrand 1976).

Meltzer, Milton. *A Book About Names*. (Crowell 1984).

Mencken, H. L. *The American Language*. (Knopf 1962).

Safire, William. *Let a Simile Be Your Umbrella*. (Crown 2001).

Stewart, George R. *American Place-Names*. (Oxford University Press 1970).

Thoreau, Henry David. *The Journals of Henry David Thoreau*. (Gibbs M. Smith 1984).

Theroux, Alexander. *The Primary Colors*. (Henry Holt 1994).

———. *The Secondary Colors*. (Henry Holt 1996).

Wells, Diana. *100 Flowers and How They Got Their Names*. (Algonquin 1997).

———. *100 Birds and How They Got Their Names*. (Algonquin 2002).

Children's Books

Belting, Natalia. *Our Fathers Had Powerful Songs*. (Dutton 1974).

Bograd, Larry. *Bernie Entertaining*. (Delacorte 1987).

Danziger, Paula. *Amber Brown* series. (Scholastic).

Graham-Barber, Lynda. *A Chartreuse Leotard in a Magenta Limousine*. (Hyperion 1995).

Hobbs, Will. *Bearstone*. (Camelot 1997).

Hurwitz, Johanna. *Hurray for Ali Baba Bernstein*. (Apple 1993).

Lee, Chinlun. *The Very Kind Rich Lady and Her One Hundred Dogs*. (Candlewick 2001).

Lee, Laura. *The Name's Familiar: Mr. Leotard, Barbie, and Chef Boyardee*. (Pelican 1999).

——— *The Name's Familiar II*. (Pelican 2001).

Lester, Julius. *Sam and the Tigers: A New Telling of Little Black Sambo*. (Dial 1966).

Lobel, Anita. *Allison's Zinnia*. (Greenwillow 1990).

———. *Away from Home*. (Greenwillow 1994).

Lowry, Lois. *Taking Care of Terrific*. (Yearling 1991).

McCord, David. *One at a Time*. (Little, Brown 1974)

Park, Linda Sue. *When My Name Was Keoko*. (Clarion 2002).

Paterson, Katherine. *The Great Gilly Hopkins*. (HarperCollins 1978).

Spinelli, Jerry. *Report to the Principal's Office*. (Econo-Clad 1999).

Terban, Marvin. *Guppies in Tuxedos: Funny Eponyms*. (Clarion 1988).

4

Prefixes, Suffixes, and Other Sacred Cows

The April 6, 1959 issue of *Life* magazine contained this observation:

> If you should ask Dr. Seuss how he ever thought up an animal called a Bippo-no-Bungus from the wilds of Hippo-no-Hungus or a Tizzle-Topped Tufted Mazurka from the African island of Yerka, his answer would be disarmingly to the point: "Why, I've been to most of those places myself, so the names are from memory. As for the animals, I have a special dictionary which gives most of them, and I just look up their spellings."

We need to take children to fantastic kingdoms and show them marvelous things; we need to expose them to wonderful words. We don't need to give children lists of prefixes and suffixes to memorize. But the mythology (from Greek *mythos* and *logos* via French *mythologie* from Late Latin *mythologia*) for drilling kids on affixes and roots is strong. As White, Yanagihara, and Sowell observed in *The Reading Teacher*, "Much of the vocabulary explosion that begins around the fourth grade is due to words with a prefix, suffix, or both." So in response, people who operate on a "get-'em-ready" notion of education decree prefixes and suffixes in second grade. Oklahoma's so-called PRIORITY ACADEMIC STUDENT SKILLS include this imperative for Grade 2: "The student will build and understand words using prefixes, suffixes, and base words." In Alabama, official documents issued by the state board of education declare that third graders *will* "interpret, evaluate, appreciate, and construct meaning from print materials using structural analysis. Examples: roots, prefixes, suffixes." Officials from Texas to Florida to Pennsylvania issue similar decrees.

And things get curiouser and curiouser. California seventh-grade students must add Anglo-Saxon roots to their repertoire having been concentrating on Latinate and Greek roots in earlier grades. This early emphasis on the Latinate is at odds with most books on improving writing, which advise choosing Anglo-Saxon words over Latinate words, imported into English in 1066 as a result of the Norman Conquest. Here are a few samples of the differences.

ENGLISH WORDS FROM ANGLO-SAXON	ENGLISH WORDS IMPORTED FROM LATIN THROUGH FRENCH
chew	masticate
die	expire
do again	repeat
do well	succeed
drink	imbibe

The Grade Five English-Arts Content Standards for California declare that fifth graders will "know abstract, derived roots and affixes from Greek and Latin and use this knowledge to analyze the meaning of complex words (e.g., *controversial*)."

Try this yourself: Figure out the meaning of *controversial* from its constituent parts.

- *con* from the Latin *contra* meaning *against*?
- *con* from the Old English meaning *to know*?
- *con* from the French *conduire*, from Latin *conducere*, meaning *conduct*?
- *trover* is from the Old French *to find*, but listed as *archaic*. Must California fifth graders be responsible for archaic?
- *contra-* is a prefix meaning *against*. The fifth grader was supposed to change the *o* to an *a*.
- *vers* is French for *verse*, coming from Latin *versus*, "turning (of a plow), furrow, line." And there is the link to *vertere*, meaning *to turn*.

The Latin *controversus* means *disputed*; literally turned against. Interesting, but to get that the fifth grader must know that *vertere* means to turn *turn*. And the fifth grader must recognize the necessity to read backward. The word does *not* mean *against turning*.

It is fascinating that *vertere* also gives us *adverse, advertise, controversy, conversation, convert, diverse, invert, obverse, pervert, prose, reverse, subvert, universe, versatile, version, versus, vertebra, vertical*, and *vertigo*. Each teacher must decide which fifth graders might find this comprehensible.

spit	expectorate
go down	descend
hate	detest
hide	conceal
high	elevated
inner	interior
motherly	maternal
sad	miserable
speed up	accelerate
watch	observe

Words having to do with bodily functions are even more dramatic in their differences. For starters, there's *kiss* and *osculate*.

One difficulty for teachers, then, is that what young children drilled in Latin and Greek roots may gain in reading (and research shows that they won't gain much) is likely to befuddle their writing. There are even more serious difficulties, which are discussed below. This student exercise from *Our Greek and Latin Roots*, by James Morwood and Mark Warman, offers first-hand, kid-friendly exposure to the difference between Anglo-Saxon and Latin-derived words.

> Write two paragraphs, telling the same story in each paragraph. In the first one, use at least five words or phrases from the first column (above). In the second paragraph, use at least five words or

Teaching Tip

There is a great deal of research showing that children cannot use conventional definitions to learn words. . . . A word's meaning needs to be contextualized, so that the learner can see how it relates to other words in a conventional spoken or written context.
—From *Reading Research to Practice: Vocabulary Development* by Steven A. Stahl

Teaching Tip

Teachers teach structural analysis because **sometimes** readers can use this information to track difficult words and approximate meanings. [emphasis added]
—From *I Read It, But I Don't Get It* by Chris Tovani

phrases from the second column. Begin the first one with "The prince hid . . .", and the second with "The prince concealed himself. . . ."

Ask students to team up with buddy readers and read their stories aloud. Then they can discuss which one they prefer, and why.

The Reality of Prefixes, Suffixes, and Other Things That Go Bump in the Night

Once Standards commissions proclaim a learning imperative, workbooks can't be far behind. "The key to vocabulary improvement is knowing the structure of words!" trumpets a workbook section on root words, prefixes, and suffixes. At first glance, the argument has plenty of appeal. Take the word stem *graph*, from the Greek *graphein*, meaning *to write*. Add the prefix *photo-*, meaning light, and the suffix *–er*, meaning *person who performs*, and you end up with *photographer*, one who makes an image on light-sensitive film. It makes a lot of sense—if you already know the meaning of the word. The eight-year-old reader trying to put all this together might well feel it would just be easier to look the word up in the dictionary.

Prefixes are typically presented in lists, along with definitions and examples.

Teaching Tip

We can—and we should—show students that knowledge of a word stem such as *graph* brings us to lots of interesting words: *autograph, biography, geography, lithograph, stenography, graphite, graphic*. But we must realize that knowledge of *graph* alone isn't going to get students to the meaning of these words. Certainly, discussion of some common prefixes and suffixes should be part of a classroom vocabulary routine. But even as we introduce the ones considered basic, we need to beware of the limitations they present. That said, *graph* words continue to multiply. *Mechanographia* entered the *Oxford English Dictionary* in June 2001.

COMMON PREFIXES

PREFIX	MEANING	EXAMPLE
bi-	two	I have a *bi*cycle.
de-	not	He will *de*bug the computer.
dis-	not	What is the *dis*advantage of this plan?
im-	not	The car was *im*mobile.
mis-	not	You *mis*understood what I said.
pre-	before	The tickets must be *pre*paid.
re-	again	We will have to *re*build the barn.
un-	not	That dress is very *un*usual.

This seems pretty straightforward, until we take a closer look and start arguing what happens when one tries to apply these definitions to words we encounter.

Prefixes

BI-

Bi- comes from the Indo-European word for *two*, and is also the ancestor of the English *two, dual*, and *binary*. *Biceps* refers to a large muscle with two points of attachment and a *bicuspid* is a tooth with two points; *bicoastal* means *of two coasts*, a *bicycle* has two wheels, and a *bikini* is a two-piece bathing suit. But bikini is named not for a two-part *kini* but for an atoll in the Marshall Islands where an atom bomb was tested in 1946.

Even though *biscuit* does come from the Latin *bis*, meaning *twice*, this information won't help readers much—unless they happen to know that the *cuit* comes from *coctus*, past participle of *coquere, to cook*. And even after knowing all that, defining *biscuit* still requires quite a stretch. *Bison* comes from a prehistoric Germanic term via Latin, and *bistro* from the French. *Bivouac* comes from German *watch* or *vigil*. And even the most word-wise person needs to double check just what *biweekly* means—both *twice a week* and *every two weeks* are in the dictionary.

A *bialy* is not a two-part *aly* but a flat, round, baked roll with small pieces of baked onion on top. This word is short for *bialystoker*, meaning *of Bialystok*, the city in Poland where this bread was made.

Teaching Tip

Asking students to find "exceptions to the rule" is an excellent technique for helping them make sense of the rule as well as helping them see that no rules are absolute, and that language rules are only as effective as the people who use them.

DE-

De- comes from Latin via an Old French word for *opposite* or *reverse*. So we get *deactivate*, *debug*, and *decapitate* (but students had better know that *caput* comes from the Latin *head* if they're trying to use their knowledge of prefixes to work this one out).

Other words beginning in *de-* offer other solutions: *dealer* comes from the Old English for *distributor*, *dearth* from the Old English for *dear* (because it is scarce); *debacle* from the French meaning tumultuous breakup of ice in a river; *debit* from the Latin *debitum* or *debt*; *debris* from the French for *broken up*; *decadence* from the Latin *decadere*, *to fall down*; *deception* from the Latin *decipere*.

Word Watch

Decrypt poses intriguing possibilities and illustrates how one word may or may not lead to another. *Crypt* comes from the Greek *krupte,* meaning *vault.* A crypt is an underground room used as a burial chamber. But *decrypt* does not mean taking a body out of a vault. *Crypto* is a prefix meaning *secret,* and *decrypt* means to decode a secret message into language people can understand. Thus the *de-* prefix is important, but the language sleuth must also sort out the various meanings of *crypt* and *crypto.*

DIS-

Dis- comes from Latin and Old French meaning literally *apart*, giving us the meaning today of *opposite*, and it is one of the more useful prefixes for young readers to know. It gives us *disability, disabuse, disadvantage, disagree, disallow, disappear, disbelief, discourteous, discover, dishonest, disintegration, dislocation, disobey, disorganize, disrespectful,* as well as many others.

Disappoint belongs in this list, but young readers are likely to be stumped by *appoint*. *Disappoint* comes from the French *desppointer*, literally *to deprive of an appointment*. Then the reader still has to unlock that to the modern meaning of *not living up to expectations*. This is clearly a case where knowing the prefix will get the struggling reader nowhere. Similarly *disburse* has an interesting history but not one a young reader is likely to be able to draw on. It comes from the Old French *desbourser*, *bourse* meaning *purse* so that it means literally *remove from the purse*.

Other words worthy of examination for figuring out how *dis-* does and doesn't help a reader unlock the meaning: *discipline, discrimination, discussion, disdain, diseased, disguise, disgust, distance, distinguish,* and *distort.*

Word Watch

Discard came into use in the mid-eighteenth century and meant *getting rid of a card,* or removing a card from one's hand and not playing it.

IM- OR IN- OR IL- OR IR-

Im-, in-, il-, and *ir-* are related to the Old English *un-*, meaning *not*. But they are also related to the French meaning *into*. So we see *inability, inaccuracy, inactive, inadvisable, inanimate, incapable*. But we also have *inaugurate, inboard, inborn, incandescence,* and so on. Definitely a puzzlement for young readers.

We have *illogical* but also *illuminate*. We have *incomplete* but also *incorporate* and *include*. Take a look at irradicate and indicate.

Prefixes, Suffixes, and Other Sacred Cows

This is not to say that knowledge of *ir-* doesn't come in handy. It helps readers unlock the meaning of *irrational, irreconcilable, irrecoverable, irredeemable,* and *irregular,* to name just a few.

Word Watch

Irrawaddy has nothing to do with the prefix *ir-*. At 1,300 miles in length, it is the principal river of Myanmar (Burma).

▌▌▌▌▌▌▌▌▌▌▌▌▌▌▌■■■■■■■

MIS-

Mis- comes from an old German word meaning *to go wrong,* and we use *mis-* to mean *badly* or *wrongly,* so that *misbehavior* means *bad behavior.* This prefix brings children to the meaning of a string of words, including: *miscommunication, misconduct, miscount, misfit, misplace, misprint,* and *misunderstand.*

Other words beginning in *mis-* have a multitude of heritages. *Miscellaneous* comes from *miscere,* meaning *to mix;* knowing that our modern word *mix* comes from this same source helps young readers remember the definition of the bigger word. *Miserable* comes from the Latin *miserabilis,* meaning *unfortunate* or *pitiable. Miser* also originates here. *Missile* comes from the Latin via French *mittere,* meaning *to send,* which is also the source of our *mission.* We sometimes refer to letters as *missives.* As further evidence that *mis-* at the beginning of a word may or may not mean *to go wrong, mister* is a courtesy title, not evidence that a *ter* has gone wrong.

Word Watch

Mississippi is a word common to several Native American languages. Eminent historian George Stewart notes that it was recorded in French in 1666 as *messipi,* or *big-river,* from the Algonquian.

▌▌▌▌▌▌▌▌▌▌▌▌▌▌■■■■■■■

PRE-

Pre- comes from the Latin meaning *before.* It is useful in figuring out such words as *preview, precaution, premature, preoccupied. Prejudice* offers opportunity for a deeper look at a word, showing children that the prefix and root travel together. When definitions trip easily off the tongues of people of all ages, extricating the *judic* (*judiciary, judicial, adjudicate, judgment*) from the word's definition makes the real meaning come alive when you put it back together.

But, as with other prefixes, *pre-* can't be taken for granted. There's *preach, precede, precedent, precept, precinct, precious, precipice, precipitation, precise, predator, predicament, preempt,* and so on. Some fit the *pre-* pattern; some don't. Let the reader beware.

Word Watch

This one is for the teachers, not for the kids. *Precocious* comes from the Latin *praecox,* literally meaning *cooked ahead.* Think of that during the next parent-teacher conference.

▌▌▌▌▌▌▌▌▌▌▌▌▌■■■■■■■

RE-

Re- is a prefix meaning *again* or *new,* and is handy for such words as *reacquaint, readjust,* and *reconnect,* but when one looks at a dictionary list of *re-* words, many seem rather odd: *replate, repledge, repot, reprivatize, resew, resocialize, resolder, respray, restress, retime, revictual.* In theory, one can add *re-* to just about anything. How often one finds a use for such words is another matter.

Another caution: *re* is also a word stem, coming from the Latin *res,* meaning *thing,* so that *real* means belonging to things, *rebus* is a word represented by things (not a new bus), *republic* is from *res public,* meaning literally *the public matter.*

UN-

Un- is a prefix meaning *do the opposite, reverse.* From *unabsorbed* to *unworkable,* readers encounter it all the time. The dictionary goes to great lengths to list words which can take this prefix, including *unyoung*, which I find *unacceptable*.

Word Watch

Undead is a word readers of vampire stories will encounter. It refers to beings who are technically dead but who still interact with the living.

▮ ▮ ▮ ▮ ▮ ▮ ▮ ▮ ▮ ▮ ▮ ▮ ▮ ▮ ▮ ▮ ▮ ▮ ▮ ▮

The Big News About Prefixes

With the cautionary message above in place, here's the big news. Some scholars declare that four prefixes account for about half the prefixed words in English. As pointed out above, the difficulty comes in recognizing when a word is prefixed and when it isn't. Here are the Big Four:

PREFIX	MEANING	EXAMPLE
dis-	not; do the opposite	dislike; disentangle
in-, im-	in, into; not	insight; incorrect, impure
re-	again; back	reappear; replace
un-	not, the opposite of	unhappy

And here are the sixteen others that along with the four above account for nearly all prefixes in English. You've met a few already, with the necessary warnings, but here they are all together.

- ab-
- ad-, ap-, at-
- bi-
- com-, con-, col-, co-
- de-
- em-, en-
- ex-
- mono-
- ob-, op-
- post-

Teaching Tip

When knowledge of only twenty prefixes can make a student prefix-proficient, it seems almost unprofessional to withhold the information. A better option is for the teacher to be ever alert for these important signals. When these prefixes occur in the reading of the day, stop occasionally and point them out. Comment on how important they are. Ask students to analyze what function they perform. Prefixes as day-to-day working knowledge beats word lists every time.

- pre-
- pro-
- sub-
- super-
- trans-
- tri-

Fortunately/Unfortunately

The good news, according to *The American Heritage Word Frequency Book*, is that the prefix *un-* accounts for 26 percent of the total of prefixed words occurring in school texts grades 3 through 9. The top four prefixes—*un-*, *re-*, and *in-* (meaning *not*), and *dis-* —account for 51 percent of the total. So we can look at this data and think that teaching just four prefixes will accomplish wonders. The not-so-good news is, as shown above, each of these prefixes has at least two separate meanings. The other difficulty, also illustrated above, is the false analysis trap. This happens when removal of the prefix leaves something weird. *Invented* is a good example. Removing *in-* leaves *vent*, a perfectly good word but one having nothing to do with the meaning of *invented*. White, Yanagihara, and Sowell report that students run into "a relatively high risk of false analysis" when dealing with *re-*, and *in-*; the risk is somewhat reduced with *dis-*.

There's more bad news. White, Yanagihara, and Sowell also report that "about three-fourths of the words beginning with the letters *re-* and *in-* are not prefixed words at all, and about half of the words beginning with *dis-* are

In "Teaching Elementary Students to Use Word-Part Clues," White, Yanagihara, and Sowell recommend teaching the nine most frequently used prefixes over a two-year period. This covers 76 percent of the prefixed words. Then teach prefixes "as the need or opportunity arises." For example, when the word *subarctic* crops up in a geography lesson, the teacher should point out the *sub-* is a prefix that means, among other things, *below*.

not true prefixed words. To make matters worse in the case of *in-*, the student must cope with alternate spellings that have the same meaning, namely, *im-*, *ir-*, and *il-*." What is a student supposed to do with, say, *intent*?

The third pitfall is that correct unlocking of prefixes can still lead to wrong definitions. *Indelicate* does not mean *not flimsy*—even though it sure looks like it should. And what about *inborn*? *Infusion*? Some scholars say that this "wrong result" happens in about 15 to 20 percent of the prefixed words kids read.

When teaching prefixes, show students a few of the words that might fool them as well as the genuine prefixed words. So in introducing *un-* they will discuss *uncle* and *unique* as well as *unhappy*.

Suffixes

Now we can move on to suffixes. Here's the way suffixes are typically presented. The reader is presented with a list, which includes an example of how the suffix works.

COMMON SUFFIXES

SUFFIX	MEANING	EXAMPLE
-able or -ible	able to	That plot was unbeliev*able*.
-er	doer	She is my favorite teach*er*.
-ful	full of	The party was delight*ful*.
-ly or -y	like; having characteristic of	Her manner was queen*ly*.
-ment	state of	There is a new housing develop*ment*.
-ness	state of being; quality	This gives me happi*ness*.
-ous	full of	The icy roads are hazard*ous*.

Now we can take a closer look.

-ABLE

The suffix *-able* (also *-ible*) comes from Middle English from French. Its meaning was capable or worthy of. The suffix is not actually related to the adjective *able*, but a word such as *eatable* is taken as *eat + able*, able to be eaten. So, too, *wearable, breakable, bearable*, and so on. Young readers are likely to encounter difficulties trying to apply this suffex. For example: *agreeable*. Yes, one meaning is *ready to consent*, but a more common meaning is *pleasing*. And what is an eight-year-old to make of *suitable*? Capable of dressing up in a suit? Capable of being brought to trial? And there's *possible*. It comes intact from the Old French and is definitely not a form of *posse*.

-ER

-Er comes from Old English and has several uses:

- to indicate a person occupationally connected: hatter, lawyer, teacher.
- to form comparative degree of adjectives and adverbs: hotter, colder, nicer.
- to indicate native of, resident of, or a person or think associated with: New Yorker, newcomer

But *-er* at the end of a word may not mean any of these things. If a *typer* is one who types, that doesn't make a *goober* one who goobs, or *cider* a comparative of cid. A *taper* may be one who tapes but that's a relatively

Word Watch

Students can discuss these words, trying to figure out which ones do and which ones don't end with the *-er* suffix. Then they can check the dictionary.

barrier	chiffonnier	plumber
badger	geyser	slander
beaver	horsepower	waiter
bumper	linebacker	writer
chapter	monster	
character	order	

■■■■■■■■■■■■■■■■■■■

Meander, another oddball *-er* word, has a fascinating history. Although it ends with *er,* that's not the *doer* suffix. The word comes from the Greek *Maiandros* via the Latin *maeander. Maiandros* is the Greek name for a river now called the Buyuk Menderes, a river in Turkey. Maiandros also referred to ornamental design popular in ancient Greek art. It is made by a continuous line that forms square shapes by doubling back on itself. Challenge students to come up with an argument for or against naming a canyon in Dead Horse Point State Park in eastern Utah *Meander Canyon.* Give extra credit if they can see a connection with ancient Greek vases.

■■■■■■■■■■■■■■■■■■■

Here's a challenge for students. Are all *nesses* "good"? Can they come up with some *-ness* words that are up to no good?

■■■■■■■■■■■■■■■■■■■

Ness also comes from the Old English *nasu* or *nose,* and from this we get names indicating capes or prominatories. It is often used at the end of place names and is also the name of a Scottish lake where a famous monster resides, Loch Ness.

■■■■■■■■■■■■■■■■■■■

new meaning. A taper with longer lineage comes to us from the Old English word for *candle.*

-FUL
-Ful comes from the Old English meaning *full of.* Over time this has come to mean *having, characterized by,* or *having the qualities of.* This gives us *beautiful, graceful, delightful, forgetful.*

-LY, -Y
-Ly and *-y* come from the Old English meaning *like in appearance, manner,* or *nature.* So we have *queenly, fatherly, gracefully, honestly, cowardly.* As always with suffixes, some words offer problems. *Seedy,* for one, can mean *full of seeds,* but how will the student get to its more general meaning of *shabby?* And how about *likely?* How does a student get to the *probably* meaning using the *-ly* rule?

-MENT
-Ment occurred originally in adopted French words. The suffix, indicating action or process, often exists as an addition to French verbs of action adopted into such English words as *abridgement, accomplishment, commencement, punishment.*

-NESS
-Ness is a suffix meaning *state, condition,* or *quality.* We see it in *happiness, pleasantness, truthfulness,* and so on. It is possible to add *ness* to any adjective or participle—or to adjective phrases, such as in *up-to-dateness.* The *Oxford English Dictionary* offers this 1888 citation from *Century Magazine:* "Cheerfulness, kindliness, cleverness, and contentedness, and all the other good nesses."

As with all prefixes and suffixes, one cannot apply rules arbitrarily. *Business* used to have one meaning, *the state or quality of being busy,* but that meaning is now considered obsolete, and *business* has acquired a host of different meanings. *Harness* is not the state of being *har* but a Middle English word meaning *gear.*

Word Watch

Here are a few interesting uncommon words with common suffixes:

- *garbology:* the study of a culture by examining what it throws away.
- *oniomania:* the urge to shop till you drop.

▮ ▮ ▮ ▮ ▮ ▮ ▮ ▮ ▮ ▮ ▮ ▮ ▮ ▮ ▮ ▮ ▮ ▮

-OUS

-Ous comes from the Latin, meaning *plentiful, full of.* So *famous* is *full of fame, adventurous* is *full of adventure,* and so on. Sometimes the *-ous* at the end of words doesn't signal a suffix. For example, *conscious* comes from the Latin *conscius, precious* from the Latin *pretiosus.* This shows us why it is counterproductive to tell children all they have to do is watch for three letters on the end of the word.

Getting to the Root of the Matter

If prefixes and suffixes are sometimes useful and sometimes iffy, roots are almost always a complex matter. And yet people writing state standards blithely declare that a third grader "will use structural analysis to identify root words." I have on my desk *The American Heritage Dictionary of Indo-European Roots* (Watkins). Let me just say, this book isn't for sissies. Nor is the *Word Parts Dictionary* (Sheehan). These and similar tomes aren't for eight-year-olds either. Although I find it fascinating to learn that *paradise, dough,* and *lady* are "ultimately derived from the same prehistoric root," I find following this path, as well as the paths of the 13,000 other English words with roots in Proto-Indo-European, tough going. I am not bothered when teachers teach root words to their students. I am bothered when they make it sound as easy as yelling "Jiminy Cricket!" to recognize these roots. Remember Jiminy Cricket? Teachers who claim word roots are easy should watch their noses.

Take *firm,* a Latin base meaning *firm* or *strong.* From it we get *confirmation, infirmity, firmament, reaffirmation,* and *affirmative.* So for learning *firm* to do any good, the student must also know *con-, in-, re-. af-, -ion, -ity, -ment,* and *-ative.* Where does one start? And is the payoff worth the effort it will take (always remembering, of course, that just because we teach it doesn't mean students will remember it)?

This is not to say that the word links with roots aren't fascinating. From the base *spir, to breathe,* we get *aspire, aspiration, conspire, conspiracy, expire, inspire, inspiration, respiration, perspiration, transpire.* Fascinating, yes. Whether it is comprehensible to someone who doesn't already know the meaning of these words is worth thinking long and hard about. Similarly, look at the *err* base (from the Latin *errare*); it means *to wander* or *stray; to make a mistake.* So we get *error, erratic, erroneous.* So far so good. But we also have *errand* and *deterrent,* entirely different kettles of fish.

One can find lists of common Latin and Greek roots. On these lists you will find things like this:

ROOT	MEANINGS	EXAMPLES
fac, fact (facere)	to make or to do	facile, factory, efficient
fer (ferre)	to bear, to produce	transfer, ferry
miss, mit (mittere)	to send	admissible, transmit, dismiss
mov, mot (movere, motus)	to move	movement, motion
port (portare)	to carry	export, portable
pos, pon (posito, ponere)	to place, to put	position, opponent

What are kids to make of *fer?* Knowing *fer* makes for a nice jump to *aquifer,* but how does *fer* get us to *conference?* What about *defer? Prefer?* Young children who look at such a list are likely to wonder about *ferrets.*

And so on and so on. Knowing these common roots does not make the meanings of new words easy to figure out. What all these complications suggest is that the study of word roots should be delayed until high school when readers have a very large vocabulary from which to draw. *Then* these connections become a whole lot easier. The push to move curriculum concepts to lower and lower grades harms the children. What is impossible in third grade is often a snap in eighth. What's the rush? There are plenty of rich, valuable, and fun things to do with words.

A commonsense approach, and one that benefits children, is to offer a few basics on affixes—and maybe on roots—but mostly to offer lots of good stories about wonderful words. Students have difficulty remembering lists of disconnected words and word parts. They don't forget stories. And there are lots of wonderful books filled with wonderful stories about words. See Chapters 3 and 6 for recommendations. Also check out *susanohanian.org* each month for word stories and activities.

Cautionary Note

Here are the topics for a series of lessons from a book on word power. The arrangements for this list are interesting and probably even useful for the word-savvy teacher. But before pasting this list into your plan book for fifteen

Read More

Diana Wells's *100 Birds and How They Got Their Names* is written for adults but plenty of the information will interest and inform children. Wells provides scientific as well as common names and fascinating facts from many cultures. For example, the *Caprimulgidae* (from the Latin *caper* = *goat* and *mulgere* = *to milk*), a bird feared by Native Americans, was described by Aristotle as sucking the milk of goats, causing the goat to go blind. In America we called these birds *whippoorwill* for the sound of their cry. This is about half the information Wells provides about this bird, and ninety-nine more are featured in the book.

Teaching Tip

Life in third grade is too short to crowd it with the study of Latin and Greek roots, except when these roots offer opportunites to tell fascinating stories about origins and connections.

Read More

In *Origins*, a two-volume set from Teachers and Writers Collaborative, Sharon R. Robinson offers an approach to word families for the teacher who is committed to deep exploration. Volume 1 is subtitled *Bringing Words to Life*; Volume 2 is subtitled *The Word Families* and each looks at word roots in depth. Robinson writes, "When students take a deep breath to make themselves look as large and fierce as possible, they experience the connect of *bold* to its root *bhel* (*to swell*) and to other words of the *bhel* word family: balloon, bulge, belly, bulky, boulder." I find this approach admirable, but also somewhat problematic. It reveals the limitations of studying word families. The teacher has to end up asking herself: What have you got when you've got kids who recognize that root *bhel*? That said, Robinson offers a serious commitment to word study that will be fun—and rewarding—for students.

days—or maybe fifteen weeks—worth of lessons, know that this list comes from a college text.

- ▣ anni, annu, enni; aut, auto; bi, bio; graph, graphy; logy, ology; ped, pod
- ▣ geo; meter; micro; phon, phono; scope; scrib, scrip; tele
- ▣ contra; dic, dict; gram; phob, phobo; spect; uni
- ▣ cent, centi; cred; dec, deca, deci; kilo; milli; port
- ▣ agog, agogue; ali; arch, archy, cracy, crat; dem, demo; glot; mon, mono; olig; oligo; theo
- ▣ anthrop, anthropo; gamy; gen; geno; heter, hetero; hom, homo; leg, legis, lex; mis, miso; poly
- ▣ aqua, aqui, astro; naut; omni; poten; sci, scio; ven, veni, vent; vid, vis
- ▣ cide; capit; corp, corpor; em, en; frater, frat; mors, mort; pathy; syl, sym, syn
- ▣ aud, audi; bene; cura; fac, fect, fic, loc, loco; man, manu; nomin, onym; pseudo
- ▣ biblio; cata; dia; epi; fin; fer; log, logo; pro
- ▣ cap, cep; derm, dermo; gnosi, gnosis; gyn, gyno; hypo; ped, pedo; ri, ridi, risi; temp, tempo, tempor; tox, toxo
- ▣ archae, archaeo; brevi; cede, ceed; chron, chrono; crypt, crypto; cycl, cyclo; duc; sequi; tain, ten, tent
- ▣ ambi; belli, bello; civ, civis; mega; pac, pax, philo, polis, post; tend, tens, tent; voc, vox

- ▣ dorm; ego, err; hyper; luc, lum; nov, peri; soph; sist, sta
- ▣ anima, animus; equi; feder, fid, fide; hypn, hypno; magna, miss, mitt; nasc, nat; pon, pos; pop

Cranberries and Other Difficulties with Word Parts

The cranberry morpheme provides a cautionary note. It is a term in linguistics denoting a morpheme without meaning. Although for practical purposes we often regard words as the basic units of grammatical structure, linguists recognize a smaller unit, the morpheme, as the smallest form with a specific meaning. In the word *trees,* for example, *tree* is regarded as a morpheme meaning, roughly, *a woody perennial plant* and *-s* a morpheme meaning *more than one.* *Cranberry* gets discussion in morphology circles because *berry* has an independent meaning and is thus a morpheme, but *cran* does not have a meaning. Linguists consider it a morpheme regardless; it just makes life simpler. Some other morphemes are also difficult. For example, *Rasp* does have meaning, but it doesn't have that meaning in *raspberry.* And a *strawberry* is not a berry that is straw. Actually, there is a relationship to *straw,* but that's another story. The point here is that kids get into all kinds of cranberry morpheme-style trouble trying to locate roots and affixes. Being able to separate a word into its constituent parts isn't of much use if you end up with nonsense.

As Easy as Apple Pie—or Pneumonoultramicroscopicsilico-volcanokoniosis

Word root fans love to demonstrate that once you know roots you know everything. Dissecting *triskaidekaphobia* is a favorite card trick. *Tris* means *three, kai* means *and, deka* means *ten,* and *phobia* means *fear.* Therefore, *triskaidekaphobia* means *fear of the number thirteen*. Next?

No one seems to ask just how often the knack for dissecting *triskaidekaphobia* might come in handy.

In the *USAFA Educator* Spring 2001, Dr. Frank Gahren provided what surely must be the penultimate lesson on word roots and affixes. Gahren says that with undergraduate students being exposed to an average of 1,200–1,500 new terms each semester, word analysis is critical. He suggests that we take a look at the longest word in the English language:

> Pneumonoultramicroscopicsilicovol-
> canokoniosis

Although at first glance the word may seem formidable, Gahren advises, "The basic principles of word analysis tell us to break down a word into prefixes, roots, and suffixes, and put them all together again to construct meaning. Following this advice, we have:

pneumono: pertaining to the lungs, as in
    pneumonia
ultra: beyond, as in *ultraviolet rays*
micro: small, as in *microscope*
scopic: from the root *skopein* (Greek) to view
    or to look at
silico: from the element *silicon*, found in
    quartz, flint, and sand
volcano: (obvious meaning)
koni: from the Greek word for *dust*
osis: a suffix meaning an illness, as in
    trichinosis

Putting this all together, we deduce that *pneumonoultramicroscopicsilicovolcanokoniosis* is a disease of the lungs caused by extremely small particles of volcanic ash and soot." Gahren is pleased to point out that this "is the exact definition from the *Oxford Dictionary of the English Language* (1998)."

Gahren adds that "Cadets who gain confidence by breaking down the largest word in our language are ready for other challenges using word analysis." And he concludes, "Vocabulary development through context and word analysis combined with sharpened previewing skills helps cadets become more efficient college readers. Better readers benefit both the Air Force Academy and the Air Force, a belief echoed in the motto of the USAFA Reading Program: 'Better Readers Are Better Leaders!' "

Depending on one's own teaching philosophy, Gahren is either very clever or maybe quite obsessive. Take your pick. That's what it means to be a teacher: picking and choosing what works for you and your students.

Here's a more kid-friendly word search for students. Invite them to research a few Greek and Roman gods—and to look for words associated with these gods that we use today.

- Achilles
- Adonis
- aegis
- amazon
- Chaos
- Chimera
- Echo
- Hercules
- Janus
- Midas
- Mars
- Narcissus
- Odysseus
- Pandora
- Sisyphus

Teaching Tip

Several studies have found that children can learn words as efficiently from having stories read to them as they can from reading stories themselves.
From *Reading Research to Practice: Vocabulary Development* by Steven A. Stahl

Word Analysis Quiz for Teachers

Take a look at the following list of words. Chances are good that you will recognize some but not others. Think about what strategies you draw upon to try to figure out the meanings of the words you don't know. If possible, persuade a friend to do the same thing. Compare notes.

1. shable, shabble
2. shab
3. Shabak
4. Shabash
5. Shabbat
6. shabbed
7. shabbaroon
8. shabby
9. shabrack, shabracque
10. shab-rag
11. shabti
12. shabub, shawbubbe
13. shabu-shabu
14. Shabzieger, Schabzieger

Here are the (jumbled) definitions. With your partner, try matching definitions to words.

1. a sabre or curved sword; any little person or thing

2. a cutaneous disease in sheep

3. dingy and faded from wear or exposure; seedy; ungenerous or dishonorable

4. modern Hebrew acronym; the division of the Israeli security service concerned with counterespionage and internal security

5. from Hindi or Urduan, "Well done!"

6. a saddle-cloth used in European armies

7. Hebrew; Sabbath

8. afflicted with scabs

9. a disreputable person, ragamuffin

10. shabby, damaged, the worse for wear

11. a figure placed in Egyptian tombs to answer by magic for the deceased when called to labor in the Fields of the Blessed

12. alleged name for the plant honesty (*Lunaria biennis*)

13. a kind of hard green cooking cheese made in Switzerland from curds and flavored with melilot

14. a Japanese dish of thinly sliced beef or pork cooked with vegetables in boiling soup

Here are a few more things to consider:

- Think about your own feelings as you tried to sort through this list.
- What strategies did you use? What happened when your strategies didn't work?
- When you got everything sorted out, how did you feel?
- Was the new information about the words worth the effort?
- How can you use any of these feelings to inform your work when you consider teaching root words and affixes?

References

Andrews, Carolyn B. and Paige P. Kimble (eds.). *Paideia*. (Scripps Howard National Spelling Bee 2001).

Ayers, Donald. *English Words from Latin and Greek Elements*, 2nd edition. (University of Arizona 1986).

Bissell, John. *The American Heritage Word Frequency Book*. (Houghton Mifflin 1972).

Blachowicz, Camille and Peter Fisher. *Teaching Vocabulary in All Classrooms*. (Prentice Hall 2001).

Brown, Roland Wilbur. *Composition of Scientific Words*. (Smithsonian Institution Press 1956).

Crystal, David. *A Dictionary of Language*. (University of Chicago 1992).

Dibbley, Dale Corey. *From Achilles's Heel to Zeus's Shield*. (Fawcett Columbine 1993).

Gahren, Frank, D.F.R. "Making Sense of Nonsense—Two Techniques to Improve Reading Comprehension." *The USAFA Educator*. Spring 2001.

Kennedy, John. *Word Stems: A Dictionary*. (SoHo 1996).

McGrath, Alister. *In the Beginning: The Story of the King James Bible and How It Changed a Nation, a Language, and a Culture*. (Doubleday 2001).

McQuain, Jeffrey and Stanley Malless. *Coined by Shakespeare*. (Merriam Webster 1998).

Man, John. *Alpha Beta: How 26 Letters Shaped the Western World*. (John Wiley & Sons 2000).

Moore, Bob and Maxine Moore. *NTC's Dictionary of Latin and Greek Origins*. (NTC 1996).

Morwood, James and Mark Warman. *Our Greek and Latin Roots*. (Cambridge 1990).

Oaknin, Marc-Alain. *Mysteries of the Alphabet*. (Abbeville Press 1999).

Robinson, Sharon R. *Origins: Bringing Words to Life*. (Teachers & Writers Collaborative 1989).

———. *Origins: The Word Families*. (Teachers & Writers Collaborative 1989).

Sheehan, Michael J. *Word Parts Dictionary*. (McFarland 2000).

Stahl, Steven A. *Reading Research to Practice: Vocabulary Development*. (Brookline 1999).

Tovani, Chris. *I Read It, But I Don't Get It*. (Stenhouse 2000).

Watkins, Calvert (ed.). *American Heritage Dictionary of Indo-European Roots*, 2nd edition. (Houghton Mifflin 2000).

Weekley, Ernest. *An Etymological Dictionary of Modern English*. (John Murray 1921; Dover 1967).

White, Thomas, Alice Yanagihara, and Joanne Sowell. "Teaching Elementary Students to Use Word-Part Clues," *The Reading Teacher* 42(4): 302, January 1989.

5

Context Clues: Cure-All or Claptrap?

In *The Naked Children* Daniel Fader pulls no punches. He asserts that in their English classes, junior high students should be learning how to read newspapers, not sitting through lessons on Shakespeare. Furthermore, he points out, "As teachers we have failed to convince children of what we ourselves do not believe—that reading is for pleasure."

Research shows that when students read for pleasure, vocabulary growth occurs. But it is still hard for state selection committees, boards of education, and teachers to let students choose their own books.

Fader notes that at the reform school where he was implementing his program of letting students choose their own books, implications of sex in a title would guarantee the popularity of any book. When a teacher saw one of his poorest readers choose *The Scarlet Letter*, he suggested that maybe the boy had mistaken the book for something else. "Ain't this the one about the whore?" asked the boy. "And don't that big 'A' stand for whore?" The teacher had to admit that this was more or less correct, and the boy insisted it was the book he wanted, refusing to be dissuaded by warnings that it was a difficult text.

Three days later, the boy showed his teacher four notebook pages. He'd filled the pages with all the words—and their definitions—he'd encountered on the first eleven pages that he didn't know. He didn't produce any more written-out definitions but, in Fader's words, "Motivated by Hawthorne's whore, he fought his way through the entire book," talking to his teacher from time to time about what was happening to Hester (and reading other, easier books all the while). In the end he concluded, "That woman, she weren't no whore."

Fader documents the difficulties Hawthorne's vocabulary poses for college students, insisting that this difficulty isn't what's important in the story about the reform school boy. What's important is "a peculiarly personal interaction between a reader and a book." What a phrase: *a peculiarly personal interaction between a reader and a book*. This interaction is different for every reader and it doesn't require that the reader know every word. In fact, as Fader remarks, "the threshold of understanding—of meaningful interaction—is surprisingly low." Inspired by a whore, a poor reader can do amazing things.

When students choose their own books, astounding things are guaranteed to happen—in vocabulary and in life.

Finding Context

Context clues prove the adage "the rich get richer." For able readers, context is everywhere, with one word leading to another and all offering rich associations; for less mature readers, many words sit in icy isolation, connecting to nothing. As always, the teacher's job is to provide the locale to make learning happen. Yes, we should make students aware of helpful strategies; "context clues" have their place. But as with all strategies, we must be ever aware of keeping context clues in their uses. Research shows that context clues only play a secondary role in reading comprehension.

Readers make enormous vocabulary growth through reading, but that is not why they read. This chapter provides helpful strategies for making the most of context. It also provides reminders backed by solid research about our need to keep focused on the donut, not the hole. Whatever strategies students employ for figuring out new words, the strategy isn't the thing. What counts is that students find pleasure in words and in so doing gain independence in meaning making.

One technique is to make vocabulary research one of the options available on a literature log form. For a given chapter, ask students to record at least three interesting or unusual words, including page number and synonym or short definition for each. Periodically, students can choose one of these words to share with the class or with their reading discussion group.

Avoiding Foolish Busy Work

Four fallacies reinforce most commercial vocabulary-enhancing products. Like diet pills, they offer false promises and undercut attempts to build good reading habits.

- there are shortcuts available to foster vocabulary growth;
- vocabulary growth is a puzzle-solving trick that can be taught;
- vocabulary savvy is measured by right and wrong answers;
- some children are "behind" and must be taught rules to help them catch up.

Teaching Tip

In addition to a formal introduction of context strategies, encourage students to create personal word lists of new words they find in interesting contexts. Here is a chart to assist students in word-gathering. Remind students that recording the source of the word is important for two reasons. They may want to go back to the word. Other students may want to take a look at how the writer used the word.

Word:
Sentence in which word appeared:
Source (where word was found):
Something special about word:
Related word(s):

No, no, no, no. Say it again: No. Sounds possible. But none of this is true. Children gain vocabulary strength by being in a reading-rich environment, not by engaging in context clue drills. The "use context clues" advice trips off all our tongues as we help children figure out the meanings of unfamiliar words. Maybe it trips off too easily. Before telling young readers to use context clues, we need to consider both the child and the advice.

◼ We are asking a reader who doesn't know the word in question to figure out the structural relationships between all the words in the passage. There's a diabolical catch-22 here: knowing which other words in a sentence might define an unknown word is obvious only to readers who already know the target word.

◼ Asking a reader to define a target word by its relationship to other words in a passage assumes this reader knows the meaning of all those "clue" words.

This is not to say we should abandon the "use context clues" advice. Rather, it is to suggest that we must keep context in its place. We need to be alert to what context clues can and cannot provide to the reader.

As a warning of how foolish and useless most prepackaged context clues material is, take a look at this exercise from the workbook for second graders that is part of the paraphernalia touted by *Open Court*, a leading reading textbook publisher.

USING CONTEXT CLUES

Practice. Write a definition for the underlined word in each sentence. Circle the context clues that helped you.

◼ The *enormous* bulldozer with its huge tires got stuck in the ice.
◼ The *route* we took to the farm was long, dusty, and full of turns.
◼ Because of its beauty, the *magnificent* painting was hung in a place of great honor.

Unfortunately, these samples pose more questions than answers. Take that *enormous bulldozer* sentence. It requires readers to know the meaning of *huge* as well as to suspend their real-world knowledge. Huge tires don't require enormous vehicles. In fact, the Big Wheeler racing car, a popular children's toy, features a small racing car sitting atop humongous wheels. Additionally, the item writer assumes that the reader will associate *enormous* with *huge*. Why not with *ice*? If the reader thought that *huge* meant slippery, then the possibilities for *enormous* change.

In the second sentence, according to the context, a *route* might be a dirty rope.

Take a look at the third sample: "Because of its beauty, the *magnificent* painting was hung in a place of great honor." Asking a novice reader to unpack the meaning of *magnificent* from clues in this sentence presumes a lot. Look at the structural assumptions—the item writer takes for granted that the reader knows that *magnificent* describes *painting* and that the reader knows that *its* refers to *painting*. Also assumed is that the reader knows the meaning of beauty and honor. And so on.

Consider the demands made by these workbook mechanics:

◼ Readers must apply the questioners' rules of sentence grammar.
◼ Readers must read with internal dictionaries in their head, defining every word as they go.
◼ Readers must realize that writers put difficult words in their work to trip up the reader, but they also offer clues for the clever reader, usually in the same sentence.

The implication is that when students sit down to read they must ask themselves, "What incomprehensible vocabulary is the writer going to deliver to me and where is the clue to figuring it out?"

This is not a message designed to encourage children to develop habits for lifelong reading.

Test prep books on vocabulary mirror vocabulary workbook exercises published as

As a struggling poet trying to make myself clear, I find it very discouraging to be accused of deliberately planning a "hidden meaning" in my reader's path, and as a struggling teacher of poetry, I try hard to ban this popular term from the classroom. From *Dancing with Words* by Judith Rowe Michaels

▮▮▮▮▮▮▮▮▮▮▮▮▮▮▮▮▮▮▮▮▮

part of reading programs. Or maybe it's the other way around. Publishing conglomerates do it all: They publish basals, they publish tests, and they publish test prep workbooks. One test prep book advises the students to "look for clues in the sentence" to find the meanings of words they don't know:

(a) The loud music *blared* from the radio.
(b) Mary's father is a *pilot,* and he flies a large jet.
(c) Marlowe had an *idea;* she gave it much thought.

Only workbook mechanics write this way.

A sure way to liven up discussion at a school board or chamber of commerce meeting is to ask those assembled to read the following paragraph and take the vocabulary quiz. Only the publisher of the vocabulary test prep guide in which this appears thinks there is one right answer for each question.

> Japan is a land with a vibrant and fascinating history, varied culture, traditions, and customs that are hundreds of years old, yet segments of its society and economy are as new as the microchips in a personal computer.
>
> In paragraph 4, what is the meaning of *vibrant*?
> a) throbbing
> b) full of activity
> c) scary
> d) interesting
>
> What is the meaning of *varied*?
> a) interesting
> b) altering
> c) different
> d) several

You Are What You Read

Children aren't going to gain much vocabulary listening to adults talk. Eighty-three percent of the words in adult conversations with children come from a bare bones lexicon of 1,000 words and this lexicon doesn't change much as the child ages. As Jim Trelease points out in *The Read-Aloud Handbook,* "Whereas an adult only uses nine rare words (per thousand) when talking with a three-year-old, you'll find three times as many in a children's book, and more than seven times as many in a newspaper." By the time a child is ten years old, adults have upped their rare word count to 11.7. If they read aloud to that child, he'd be hearing 30.9 rare words per thousand.

The chart shown below of "rare words per 1000" (Hayes & Ahrens 1988) shows the oral language of college graduates as the low—17.3 rare words per 1000, and the abstracts of scientific articles as the high—128 rare words per 1000. Most provocatively, we see that TV cartoons rate higher than prime-time TV and comic books introduce more new words than do adult books. Surely this is a mandate for reading aloud to children—and making sustained silent reading an essential part of the classroom. And bring in the comic books for vocabulary enhancement!

college graduates	17.3
scientific articles	128.0
adult books	52.7
comic books	53.5
children's books	30.9
cartoon shows	30.8
prime-time adult TV shows	22.7

In *The Spying Heart,* Newbery and Hans Christian Andersen medalist Katherine Paterson offers another imperative on the best way to teach children.

> First, we must love music or literature or mathematics or history of science so much that we cannot stand to keep that love to ourselves. Then when the energy

and enthusiasm and enormous respect for the learner, we share our love.

When adults surround the children in their care with wonderful words, children come to know and to love these words.

Make Vocabulary Instruction Strategic

When students face reading with difficult vocabulary, longtime teacher Suzanne Barchers offers a vocabulary rating chart as a prereading strategy:

> The teacher gives students a list of words and the categories. Students check off each word in the applicable column before they read the selection. They then can compare their lists in small groups and speculate on alternative meanings. After they have completed their reading, they return to the sheet, with a different-colored pen or pencil, check off words they can now define. This activity does not directly teach vocabulary, but it introduces unfamiliar words, builds on existing knowledge, and generates interest in the reading.

An important part of this strategy is giving students time to talk about the vocabulary. The words below are from a fifth-grade social studies book.

VOCABULARY	CAN DEFINE	HAVE SEEN OR HEARD	NOT SURE
immigrant			
ancestor			
diversity			
customs			
survival			
pluralistic			
prejudice			
communication			

Sound and Pictures

Some students find creating mneumonic devices helpful. And those who like to draw

Teaching Tip

Text comprehension requires a deeper knowledge of words than much vocabulary instruction provides. In *Invitations,* Regie Routman cautions that vocabulary is related to concepts and should not be introduced in isolation. "Vocabulary is developed during or after reading when semantic relationships can be made. The only time I introduce a word before reading is if understanding a particular word is critical for comprehending the passage."

can add cartoons to give further punch to these devices. Humor usually helps any enterprise, including vocabulary building.

Vocabulary Cartoons: Building an Educated Vocabulary with Visual Mnemonics by Sam, Max, and Bryan Burchers promises "SAT Word Power," and the device they use will appeal to plenty of word sleuths. The authors encourage students trying to learn difficult vocabulary to associate each word with something they already know, and to draw a cartoon as a reminder. For example, *incite,* meaning arouse to action, has the mnemonic link *fight* and a cartoon caption "The pitcher's bean ball *incited* the batter to *fight.*" *Abhor,* meaning to hate very much, has the mnemonic link *chore* and a cartoon caption "The Booker boys *abhorred* doing *chores.*"

Here are a few more of the associations. Each is accompanied by a silly illustration.

- The little leaguers *beleagurered* the *big leaguers.*
- The boy's locker room showers were a *milieu* of *mildew.*
- Doctors could never *fathom* the reason for Larry's *fat thumb.*
- An *elfin elephant* is a strange sight to see.

It's definitely worth offering mneumonics to those who want to try it.

Word Jam: An Electrifying, Mesmerizing, Gravity-Defying Guide to a Powerful and Awesome Vocabulary by basketball great Walt "Clyde" Frazier features what he calls power

Remind yourself often that you cannot teach every unfamiliar word in a selection you assign students to read. Be selective. Choose the important ones. Skip other important ones. More intensive examination of a few words is more interesting—and productive—for students than being required to memorize lots of definitions.

words and frenetic graphics. The words are featured in a short story, so the words appear in context, accompanied by a humorous illustration. This is followed by word definition, derivation, and synonyms. The style is lively and kid-friendly. Here's a sample:

> *Rabid*, a word used to describe some sports fans, comes from the Latin word *rabidus*, which means *mad*. (Not *angry* mad—*nutty* mad!) And speaking of nutty . . .

> *Zany* means *funny in a crazy way*. It comes from *zanni*, the Italian word for clown.

> *Jubilant*, which means *very happy*, comes from the Latin *jubilare*. It's similar to an old German word *ju*, which means *joy*, and the Greek *iyge*, which means *shout*.

What Do We Tell Our Students?

As with so much in our craft, we are faced with balancing the problems of strategy overload with those of undernourishment. Words-in-context strategies are useful but not sufficient to reading competence. Probably the most important advice we can give children when they encounter an unfamiliar word in their reading is, "Don't stop. Keep reading."

Here are a couple of samples to show children why often they can keep reading and still understand the story.

> "Which person," she said, her voice shaking, "which *abysmally* foolish person wrote down this week's passwords and left them lying around?"
> —From *Harry Potter and the Prisoner of Azkaban* by J. K. Rowling

> Finally, there was a chink of coin passing from paw to paw, the field-mouse was provided with an *ample* basket for his purchases, and off he hurried, he and his lantern.
> —From *The Wind in the Willows* by Kenneth Grahame

And in my imagination I have answers to the *pertinent* questions.
> —From *Whale Talk* by Chris Crutcher

We must remind ourselves, "Don't stop them. Let them keep reading." If children gain some vocabulary but never enter the kingdom of people who love to read, then we have failed.

That said, helping students increase their word knowledge is important and teaching context clues is also important. *How* context is important emerges from reading a few hundred children's books. Context categories become apparent; the categories can be transformed into strategies for helping children strengthening their word knowledge and their comprehension. We must keep in mind that the strategy is what we're teaching, not the particular vocabulary in the samples. Any context sample will not be adequate for teaching a concept. The goal in using the

Writing in the *Journal of Adolescent and Adult Literacy*, Mellinee Lesley describes a practice she instituted in a developmental reading skills course at Eastern New Mexico University.

Every class period, we concluded with a summary of what we did on one side of an index card and what we learned on the other side. These cards not only helped students distill key ideas and recall class events, but also served as data for me. With the cards, my students were able to give me continual and instant feedback on each class. I was also able to monitor my students' literacy development (e.g., questioning, reflection, analysis, rising consciousness) through their observations of the class.

Apply this tip to vocabulary learning. At the end of the day ask students to write a word they learned that day. Ask them to write something about that word.

samples is not to increase students' vocabulary by a certain number of words but helping children learn to use strategies so they can gain independence in their reading.

1. The teacher introduces a strategy, demonstrating how she uses it while reading. She encourages students to listen in as she thinks aloud.

2. Students try out the strategy, with the teacher and with each other. During this trying out period, students also think out loud.

3. Students try out strategies on their own, checking in with the teacher and with other students.

4. Encourage students to use target words in sentences of their own. To know a word, students need to be able to use it.

The goal is for readers to use these strategies automatically, sifting, discarding, applying, combining, and moving on. Ask students to watch out for good examples of a strategy in their own reading. They can demonstrate the strategy for other students and then post the passage from which they gleaned the strategy on a "strategy wall." They can also add to the context clue bank, a storehouse of passages that allows students to practice their context strategies. But learning the strategies can be excruciating if the strategies are introduced as so much workbook drill. As William Nagy observes in *Teaching Vocabulary to Improve Reading Comprehension*, a little common sense goes a long way. "I would rather have students spend a few seconds looking at a picture of an armadillo than have them practice using the word *armadillo* in a sentence."

In our classroom, Emily never asks questions and when asked if she has any questions, smiles and shakes her head. Even though I know better, I plead with her, "Emily, *please* ask me for help when you don't understand something. That's what I'm here for—to help you." Emily doesn't need this friendly, vague prompting. How can she ask for help when she doesn't know what she doesn't know? As she learns to think aloud, to talk about her reading as she reads, Emily gains confidence. Emily can find one word in a paragraph that is more troubling than other words, and over time she begins to find relationships between words in the paragraph. The day she raises her hand and complains, "I don't get this," showing me a specific word, I know that strategy work has given Emily a voice in our classroom—and in her reading.

Strategy 1: Readers draw on what they know about language to figure out a new word.

This point can't be emphasized too much. Readers need to be reminded that they bring lots of information to what they are reading, and what they already know helps them learn more.

> "Amos, help me," said the mountain of a whale to the *mote* of a mouse.
> —From *Amos & Boris* by William Steig

When third graders unpacked this sentence by telling what they knew about whales and mice, *huge* and *smart* appeared on the whale list, *small* and *dirty* on the mouse list. Then readers noticed the "*mountain* of a whale" and decided *mote* must mean *small*. They were impressed and even amazed. Third graders love practicing literary constructions, and for about a week would break into whatever was going on with another contribution: "a mountain of a school bus" and "a mote of a backpack"; "a mountain of

Teaching Tip

When we tell students to draw on what they know, we should be sure to include their world. When I asked Miafra, not rated as an excellent reader, how she knew the meaning of *quest*, she told me, "Johnny Quest is on Saturday morning cartoons."

broccoli" and "a mote of ice cream." As ever, Dougie found a way to personalize it to the teacher: "You wouldn't give us a mountain of math when we only had a mote of riddle reading, would you?"

Strategy 2: Look for a definition of the word.

Sometimes authors define a word. When they do this, it is a clue for readers to pay close attention: This word is important. This strategy is often found in nonfiction. Mark Kurlansky gives not only a definition but also the derivation and further explanation.

> A group of fish is called a *school*. This is not because it is a place of learning. It is an old word from Holland that means a crowd. Fish live in crowds.
> —From *The Cod's Tale* by Mark Kurlansky

This technique is often used in textbooks and in other nonfiction. And it is also used in fiction.

> "A *Muggle*," said Hagrid, "it's what we call nonmagic folk like them. An' it's your bad luck you grew up in a family o' the biggest Muggles I ever laid eyes on."
> —From *Harry Potter and the Sorcerer's Stone*
> by J. K. Rowling

Alert students to other stylistic devices used in offering definitions. Sometimes authors anticipate the reader's not knowing a word and follow the word with a definition, set off by commas. Point out that when authors define words they are signaling that the word is important, something the reader needs to know to understand the subject matter being discussed. Often these words are also found in a textbook's glossary.

> *Palentologists*, the scientists who study fossils to learn about the history of life on Earth, would be thrilled to have such a complete skeleton to study.
> —From *A Dinosaur Named Sue: The Story of the Colossal Fossil* by Pat Relf

Traditionally, much vocabulary teaching has involved the use of definitions. We recog-

nize both their uses and their limitations. Definitions are essential but far from sufficient information. William Nagy, in *Teaching Vocabulary to Improve Reading Instruction*, observes that the glossaries in basal readers and in dictionaries don't offer enough information to allow a person to use the word correctly. Nagy clarifies the point: "One can think of it this way: Why isn't a glossary of biological terms an adequate substitute for a biology textbook? The answer in part is that important information about biological concepts and their interrelations simply does not fit into definitions." He concludes, "Reading comprehension depends on a wealth of encyclopedic knowledge and not merely on definitional knowledge of the words in the text."

A definition might give a clue, but the reader still isn't going to have a feel for Muggles until and unless he encounters them many times again. Students will learn what a palentologist is not by reading the dictionary definition but by becoming immersed in texts about what palentologists do.

Strategy 3: Look carefully at the sentence before and after the word in question.

Sometimes the surrounding words give a pretty good clue to a difficult word's meaning. You may need to read the whole paragraph very carefully. Remember, sometimes the helpful context comes before the word, and sometimes it comes afterward.

> "Oh, Mom, can I go on the train and see him, Mom, ooh please. . . ."
> "You've already seen him, Ginny, and the poor boy isn't something you *goggle* at in a zoo."
> —From *Harry Potter and the Sorcerer's Stone*
> by J. K. Rowling

So the [toy] mouse and his child danced under the tree every evening, and every night when the family was asleep they talked with the other toys. The monkey complained of being made to play the same tune over and over on a cheap fiddle; the bird complained of having to peck at a bare floor; the rabbit complained that there was no meaning in his cymbals. And soon the mouse and his child complained of the *futility* of dancing in an endless circle that led nowhere.

—From *The Mouse and His Child*
by Russell Hoban

[Scene: two men fighting.] Down went the boaster to the floor with a sounding thump, and the fickle people yelled and laughed themselves purple; for it was a new sight to see Eric of Lincoln eating dust. But he was up again almost as soon as he had fallen, and right quickly retreated to his own ringside to gather his wits and watch for an opening. He saw instantly that he had no easy *antagonist*, and he came in cautiously this time. . . . The beggar stood sturdily in his tracks contenting himself with beating off the attack. For a long time their blows were like the steadily crackling of some huge forest fire.

—From *Robin Hood and His Merry Outlaws*
by J. Walker McSpadden

Strategy 4: Try to get a feel whether the word is positive or negative.

Sometimes the context does not supply a synonym for the word in question but it does help the reader get a sense of whether the word is describing something nice or something not nice.

Many animals communicate to warn one another of danger. When every member of a group watches out for *predators*, they are all more likely to survive.

—From *Slap, Squeak and Scatter: How Animals Communicate* by Steve Jenkins

The giant became madder than a rained-on rooster. In a *tantrum*, he stomped his feet so hard the vibrations went all the way to California (where some folks say they are shaking things up still).

—From *Look Out, Jack! The Giant Is Back!*
by Tom Birdseye

The rooster charged at her, rapped her *viciously*—as if beating her for having got herself beaten.

—From *Along Came a Dog*
by Meindert DeJong

Indeed, by the next morning Harry and Ron thought that meeting the three-headed dog had been an excellent adventure and they were quite *keen* to have another one.

—From *Harry Potter and the Sorcerer's Stone*
by J. K. Rowling

Agent McLoughlin quickly decided to notify his Indian policemen that Sitting Bull was not to be allowed to leave Standing Rock, ordering them to arrest the chief. These policemen were known to the people of the tribe as Metal Breasts, for the shiny badges they wore. Sitting Bull's followers were quite *disdainful* of them, for they had chosen the white man's ways. They had become farmers, and received good salaries and fancy uniforms from the government. Most of the people, however, held on to the dream that Sitting Bull would lead them back to that cherished ancient way of life.

—From *Wounded Knee* by Neil Waldman

Strategy 5: Take a look at word parts.

Here's where knowledge of prefixes, suffixes, and roots comes in handy.

One afternoon I fell asleep in a mossy glade. I awoke to a *malodorous* sniffling and snorting. [mal + odor + ous]

—From *Bewildered for Three Days:
As to Why Daniel Boone Never Wore His Coonskin Cap* by Andrew Glass

Workmen began *dismantling* the statue for transport to America in January 1885. Every piece of metal was marked to show its position in the statue, and liberty's parts were packed into 214 crates. [dis + mantle + ing]

—From *Liberty* by Lynn Curlee

"You'd have thought Black and Potter were brothers!" chimed Professor Flitwick. *"Inseparable!"* [in + separate + able]

—From *Harry Potter and the Prisoner of Azkaban* by J. K. Rowling

Sometimes the image surrounding the word in question is so strong students may well line up for the book. Certainly they'll never forget the image.

The men were parched by the burning heat and suffered from *intolerable* thirst. Some sucked on musket balls or pebbles to stimulate saliva. Finding himself miles from water, Townsend became so thirsty that he thrust his head into a freshly killed buffalo and drank its heart blood with the other men.

—From *Townsend's Warbler*
by Paul Fleischman

Note: This is one of the most misunderstood, misused strategies. Word affixes make the most sense to people who already know the meanings of the words. For those who don't have a clue what the word means, unpacking the various parts can be problematic (see Chapter 4).

Strategy 6: Think about where you've seen the word before.

This is where a vocabulary notebook comes in handy. By the time you've written a word down several times, from various sources, a context will emerge. But even if you haven't written it down, these multiple encounters are what enrich our vocabulary banks.

All along the meadow where the cows *grazed* and the horses ran, there was an old stone wall.

—From *Frederick* by Leo Lionni

The cows are dreaming that summer is here, and they are *grazing* in the fields.

—From *The Tomten*
adapted by Astrid Lindgren

Strategy 7: Sometimes familiar words have new meanings.

The repaired alarm clock rang at six o'clock the next morning. Harry turned it off quickly and dressed silently. He mustn't wake the Dursleys. He *stole* downstairs without turning on any of the lights.
—From *Harry Potter and the Sorcerer's Stone*
by J. K. Rowling

Captain gave out hooks and line today that we might *employ* when we are not busy with the care of the ship. Ship's cook, Mr. Thompson, is willing to prepare whatever we catch.

—From *Stowaway* by Karen Hesse

Strategy 8: Be aware that sometimes no strategies work.

Sometimes the word is just there—to be puz-zled over, admired, questioned, or ignored, depending on the reader. And that's okay. Good stories, after all, are to be taken whole; they aren't written to be vocabulary lessons. Beatrix Potter, for one, can be counted on offering at least one impossible word per story. Squirrel Nutkin, for example, "was excessively impertinent in his manners." When her publisher objected, Potter insisted that children like an impossible word occasionally.

It is said that the effect of eating too much lettuce is *soporific*.
—From *The Tale of the Flopsy Bunnies*
by Beatrix Potter

A herd of waterbuck and impala antelope and about sixty *reticulated* giraffes had been our neighbors for many years.
—From *Born Free* by Joy Adamson

A week passed, and one morning when Albert opened his mouth, he peeped. The father cardinal looked at him *askance*. But Albert peeped *insistently*.
—From *Albert* by Donna Jo Napoli

One day Leonore fell ill of a *surfeit* of raspberry tarts and took to her bed.
—From *Many Moons* by James Thurber

Then Cornelius, the oldest of all the elephants, speaks in his *quavering* voice: "My good friends, we are seeking a King."
—From *Babar* by Jean de Brunhoff

The fury of the storm drove him back into the passageway; he hung on to the stair rail and peered into the black *void*.
—From *The Black Stallion* by Walter Farley

Teaching Tip

One way to help students figure out how to use context is to put sentences on an overhead, covering up the target word. Invite students to figure out what word would make sense there. Tell them to be sure and read what comes before and after that space. Remind them that they need to think about what they know as well as about what the writer has written. Encourage discussion of the volunteered words. Why was this word suggested? Does this make sense? Why or why not?

Teaching Tip

Voices in the Park by Anthony Browne, a picture book for all ages, provides a unique demonstration of the importance of context. Four people enter a park, and through their eyes the reader sees four very different visions of the world.

For adult reading, the ultimate "context" reading with a variety of points of view is Raymond Queneau's classic *Exercises in Style.* First published in 1947, Queneau describes the same scene ninety-nine times. A book that can be enjoyed on many levels, some of it is accessible to children—and they love the very notion.

Words in Context Bank

The appendix contains a *Words in Context Bank* that provides passages illustrating the eight words in context strategies. The passages are in random order, not matched up neatly by strategy. These passages can be used in a variety of ways:

- Use one a day for whole-class consideration.
- Assign different passages to small groups, with each group presenting its solution to the class along with an explanation.
- Make them available for individual work. The range of difficulty makes the passages useful both for students who need extra help and for those wanting an extra challenge.
- Introduce longer passages so that students realize that context comes in chunks and are more than looking for a single clue.
- Be sure to ask students to replenish the words in context bank with passages from their reading.

Above all, remember that word study should result in a joy of discovery, an appreciation and love for words. These words are offered as possibilities for an ongoing discussion of the wisdom, whimsy, and wealth of words, not as items for drill.

Wondrous Words

On his homepage (*http://smallworld.sociology.columbia.edu/~dodds/wordsmithery/dictionary.html*), Columbia University Professor Peter Dodds has compiled a Trictionary, a collection of words of interesting meanings, peculiar origins, some for which he finds the enunciation simply a physical pleasure.

These are commendable categories to consider for personal word collections:

Interesting Words
Weird Words
Words That Feel Good to Say

In an interview with Bill Moyers, poet Coleman Barks defines poetry as "a delight with language," recalling that when he was about twelve he started keeping a notebook. "I wrote down words that I loved the taste of, words such as *azalea*, or for some reason *halcyon* . . . and words like *jejune* . . . I was a collector of odd words . . . language that is delicious to the mouth."

Just for the Fun of It

Andrew Clements's *Double Trouble in Walla Walla* immerses students in words that are fun to say. On an ordinary Monday morning in Walla Walla, Lulu starts the whole school talking in a higgledy-piggledy chitter-chatter. Pretty soon all the razzmatazz gives the adults the heebie-jeebies—even though they're talking this way too. From hubba-hubba to ooey-gooey to turkey-lurkey to vroom-vroom, there's page after page of achey-breaky kind of hanky-panky. Once kids have read it aloud, they will find lots of similar expressions that didn't get into the book. And remember, you can borrow the concept even if you don't have the book.

Invite students to read the words for the sheer fun of it. Challenge them to develop their own hubba-hubba lists. In *Reading Without Nonsense*, Frank Smith points out that by the time children get to school, they know an average of 20,000 words. They didn't learn these words by looking them up in the dictionary, by examining their prefixes and suffixes, or being quizzed on them once a week. They achieved this vocabulary by exclaiming "E-I-E-I-O!" and "I'll huff and I'll puff and I'll blow your house in!" Going to school shouldn't mean leaving word antics behind. In the words of a *Miami Herald* headline in May 2002, "Hubba hubba." They were cheering the Hubble Space Telescope. We can cheer children's love of words.

Finding Words— and Keeping Them

Teachers find their authority to teach vocabulary in their own love of words. Never was the adage "you reap what you sow" more true than in the vocabulary garden you cultivate in your classroom. Don't tell students you love words. Show them! Surround them with words you find fascinating. Mostly you'll do this one word at a time, but remember to leave room for lists. Lists of things you love; lists of things you detest. Lists of "just because" words that catch your fancy at this moment.

We need to be reminded that although context is often important, sometimes it is irrelevant. The words below show us that sometimes the word all by itself is plenty. We don't know what special meanings these words have for the list maker; the words draw us in, persuading us to supply our own contexts, personal and peculiar. The words, devoid of context, work a magic simply by their presence.

Invite students to read the list aloud to a buddy. Invite them to enjoy the words for their sound, the images they provoke, the memories they call up, for the company they keep on the list. Let this list be an inspiration for you to start—or add to—your own word list to share with students. Encourage students to do the same.

adagio	illuminate	quilted
Appaloosa	iridescent	ridiculous
bamboozle	jalopy	rockabilly
bumblebee	juxtapose	saxophone
cobra	king-size	sesame
cumulus	kudos	trapeze
daffodil	ladybug	tyrannosaurus
delicious	larynx	umbrella
Ecuador	moose	unicorn
elusive	mythology	vamoose
felicity	namby-pamby	vanquish
forsooth	niche	whimsy
gallop	ochre	whippoorwill
gargoyle	opossum	yada yada yada
hippopotamus	peony	yikes
hyperbole	putrid	zenith
icicle	Quebec	zucchini

References

Adult Books

Barchers, Suzanne. *Teaching Reading: From Process to Practice*. (Wadsworth 1997).

Burchers, Sam, Max, and Bryan. *Vocabulary Cartoons: Building an Educated Vocabulary with Visual Mnemonics*. (New Monic Books 1997).

Fader, Daniel. *The Naked Children*. (Macmillan 1971).

Frazier, Walt. *Word Jam: An Electrifying, Mesmerizing, Gravity-Defying Guide to a Powerful and Awesome Vocabulary*. (Troll 2001).

Hayes, D.P. and M.G. Ahrens. "Vocabulary Simplification for Children: A Case of 'Motherese'." *Journal of Child Language* 37: 395–410, 1988.

Lesley, Mellinee. "Exploring the Links Between Critical Literacy and Developmental Reading." *Journal of Adolescent and Adult Literacy* 45: 180, November 2001.

Michaels, Judith Rowe. *Dancing with Words*. (NCTE 2001).

Moyers, Bill. *Fooling with Words: A Celebration of Poets and Their Craft*. (Harper 2000).

Nagy, William. *Teaching Vocabulary to Improve Reading Comprehension*. (NCTE 1989).

Paterson, Katherine. *The Spying Heart*. (Lodestar 1989).

Routman, Regie. *Invitations*. (Heinemann 1994).

Smith, Frank. *Reading Without Nonsense*. (Teachers College Press 1997).

Queneau, Raymond. *Exercises in Style*. (New Directions 1947).

Trelease, Jim. *The Read-Aloud Handbook*, 5th edition. (Penguin 2001).

Children's Books

Adamson, Joy. *Born Free*. (Shocken 1960; 2000).

Birdseye, Tom. *Look Out, Jack! The Giant Is Back!* (Holiday House 2001).

Browne, Anthony. *Voices in the Park*. (DK Publishing 1998).

Brunhoff, Jean de. *Babar*. (Random House 1966).

Clements, Andrew. *Double Trouble in Walla Walla*. (Millbrook 1997).

Crutcher, Chris. *Whale Talk*. (Greenwillow 2001).

Curlee, Lynn. *Liberty*. (Atheneum 2000).

DeJong, Meindert. *Along Came a Dog*. (Harper 1980).

Farley, Walter. *The Black Stallion*. (Random 1991).

Fleischman, Paul. *Townsend's Warbler*. (HarperCollins 1992).

Glass, Andrew. *Bewildered for Three Days: As to Why Daniel Boone Never Wore His Coonskin Cap*. (Holiday House 2000).

Grahame, Kenneth. *The Wind in the Willows*. (Simon & Schuster 1989).

Hesse, Karen. *Stowaway*. (Simon & Schuster 2000).

Hoban, Russell. *The Mouse and His Child*. (Arthur A. Levine 2000).

Jenkens, Steve. *Slap, Squeak and Scatter: How Animals Communicate*. (Houghton Mifflin 2001).

Kurlansky, Mark. *The Cod's Tale*. (Putnam 2001).

Lindgren, Astrid. *The Tomten*. (Paper Star 1997).

Lionni, Leo. *Frederick*. (Knopf 1987).

McSpadden, J. Walker. *Robin Hood and His Merry Outlaws*. (World Publishing 1946).

Napoli, Donna Jo. *Albert*. (Silver Whistle 2001).

Potter, Beatrix. *The Tale of The Flopsy Bunnies*. (Frederick Warne 1909).

Relf, Pat. *A Dinosaur Named Sue: The Story of the Colossal Fossil*. (Scholastic 2000).

Rowling, J. K. *Harry Potter and the Prisoner of Azkaban*. (Scholastic 2001).

———. *Harry Potter and the Sorcerer's Stone*. (Scholastic 1999).

Steig, William. *Amos & Boris*. (Farrar, Straus, and Giroux 1971).

Thurber, James. *Many Moons*. (Harcourt 1981).

Waldman, Neil. *Wounded Knee*. (Atheneum 2001).

6

Word Play for Fun and Fundamentals

Fun is fundamental is a precept to teach by. The roots are in Deuteronomy: Man doesn't live by bread alone. So, too, children can't live by a so-called scientific reading method. Word *play* is fundamental for vocabulary development. The word itself provides the clue: *fun*damental begins with fun. Word play is not a trivial pastime. Anthropological linguist Peter Farb insists that play and games are "two of life's very serious and complex activities."

More than twenty years of playing word games with students ranging from grade one through college convinces me that when the fun is missing from the fundamentals, the fundamentals never stick. One year, when I had taken a leave of absence, the district called me back to replace a seriously ill reading teacher. That school's reading curriculum was DISTAR (recently renamed direct instruction). Never having done it, I agreed to try it. I got through four days and then told the principal that to continue teaching, I needed to see each student group for an extra period—to show them the way language really works. Because the ailing teacher had a light load, by meeting one group of first graders during lunch, I was able to provide each group of children the necessary fun in fundamentals. To do less would have been malpractice.

Riddle Making

Riddles, of course, depend on understanding and appreciating words' double meanings. That's why homonyms, homographs, homophones, and idioms are a staple of riddle production. Genre riddle collections, that is, riddles gathered around one subject, have great value for young readers. Such riddles, read and groaned over en masse, demonstrate how language works; they also demonstrate that language is communal, that riddle writers borrow from and build upon others' work.

> Why did the turkey cross the road?
> *To show he wasn't chicken.*

Such a riddle acknowledges young readers as intellectuals. After all, to find humor here the eight-year-old must recognize the idiom "to be chicken" and must also recognize classic riddle tradition, understanding that this riddle refers to "Why did the chicken cross the road?" When the reader gets the turkey joke, then he's ready for the question, "Why didn't the dinosaur cross the road?" Young children are thrilled to be invited into this cerebral tradition, and older kids appreciate the variations they can create.

When Tom read that the ostrich crossed the road for the same reason as the chicken—to get to the other side—he protested that the riddle writer was cheating. But as he read more, he began to enjoy the borrowings and the variations on a theme. Tom began collecting "cross the road" riddles:

Why did the worm cross the road?
To get away from the chicken.

Why did the grizzly cross the road?
It was the chicken's day off.

Why did the sheep cross the road?
It needed to make a ewe turn.

Why did the dinosaur cross the road?
There weren't any chickens back then.

Why didn't the dinosaur cross the road?
Because there were no roads back then.

Day after day, Tom stood up in front of the class during our riddle presentation time at the end of the day and told a "cross the road" riddle. And then, Tom made up his own riddle:

Why didn't the mummy cross the road?
He was all tied up.

A teacher's dream. Not only did Tom create something, his riddle forged new ground for his classmates, drawing on an idiomatic expression "all tied up." (See pp. 97–104 for the link between idioms and riddles.) Tom is playing with words. He is also working hard, using riddles as a vehicle for learning how language works. It doesn't hurt that his efforts elicit laughter from his classmates and his teacher.

Bernard Most's *Moo-Ha!* is a board book, its sturdy cardboard pages intended for toddlers. But the simple idea serves older children well as an introduction to writing riddles. Since it's not advisable to take a book for the "children under three" set into your middle grades classroom, just take the idea. Bernard Most asks a simple question: What makes a cow laugh? And then he provides an answer on each page:

moosepapers
amoosement parks
mooseums
visiting Moo York City
moovies

Aspiring riddle writers will see that each of these "moo" expressions can stand as the answer to a riddle:

Where did the cow go on his vacation?
Moo York City

Once students get the idea, they can consult dictionaries and atlases and come up with all sorts of variations on this one riddle. That cow can also go to Moo Jersey, Moo Mexico, Moo Orleans, and so on. What a way to learn geography! Linguistic sophisticates will figure out that words like *Newton*, *nuclear*, and *nutrient* also work. With the latter two it's sound that counts, not spelling. Students can also consider *moonlight*, *moonshine*, and other *moon* words.

A reviewer lauded Most's book for being fun "even though it's not educational." According to my dictionary, *to educate* is to stimulate or develop mental growth. For the right kid at the right time, I can't think of anything more educational than this clever little book.

Daffy Dinosaurs

I picked up Bernard Most's *If the Dinosaurs Came Back*, knowing my third graders would

Read More

Unfortunately, many of the classic riddle collections are out of print, but Katy Hall and Lisa Eisenberg have written a series of satisfying genre riddle books that have staying power: *Batty Riddles, Buggy Riddles, Bunny Riddles, Chickey Riddles, Creepy Riddles, Fishy Riddles, Grizzly Riddles, Kitty Riddles, Mummy Riddles, Puppy Riddles, Sheepish Riddles, Snakey Riddles,* and *Spacey Riddles.* Children who read these riddles will gain appreciation for homonyms, learn how important spelling is, boost their vocabulary, and have a great time.

Where Did the Rabbit Pilot Land?

Here's a technique for writing riddles that will quickly make you a riddle champ.

1. Find a synonym for the subject. With rabbit we have *bunny* and *hare*. We choose hare because it has lots of possibilities for "sound alike" words.

2. Find all the words that begin with the *hare* sound, or something close. Here we can use words that drop the *h* in the sound because they are close enough to make the joke work:

   hare
   hair
   air
   heir
   ere
   err

3. This becomes your word bank. Use these words and try to branch out. Look at famous place names with the *hare/air* sound: *cities, states, countries, airports, buildings*

   Where did the rabbit pilot land?
   O'Hare Airport in Chicago.

or

   Where did the rabbit pilot land?
   Kennedy Hareport in New York

4. Note that you find the answer before you ask the question. Once you realize that *hareport* will work, than lots of riddle questions are possible.

5. Your turn. Make a list of possible places where the rabbit can do something.

6. Next try to associate the *hare/air* sound with famous people.

   Who was a famous rabbit pilot?
   Amelia Harehart.

7. Next try to associate the *hare/air* sound with occupations. Use a dictionary to help you get ideas.

   An aeronautical engineer could become . . .

   An aerobics trainer would . . .

8. Bonus: Can you create a rabbit-related riddle based on an idiom?

Where Did the Pig Go on Vacation?

1. Try the same technique you learned with rabbit/hare with pig.

2. Find some synonyms for *pig.* Hint: More than one word works.

3. Create a word bank by finding words with the sound of your synonym.

4. Look for the names of places, people, and occupations that you can associate with your synonym. These become your riddle answer.

5. Ask the riddle question to go with your answer.

6. Bonus: Can you create a pig riddle related to a popular song?

7. Bonus: Can you create a pig riddle based on an idiom or a proverb?

love it. But at the last minute, instead of showing them the book, I gave them a homework assignment: "If the dinosaurs came back, what would you do? What would they do?" The responses were disappointing, bland, colorless, and dull:

- I'd ask him to be my friend.
- I'd make him my pet.
- I'd run fast.

All except Steve. I could never remember the name of his Boston-diagnosed learning disability as long as my arm, but daily, as I watched Steve struggle with getting letters going in the right direction, I had evidence of what it meant. This assignment was ideal for Steve—he could show his wit and creativity without having to write much. His two (misspelled) words, wonderfully apt and original, reminded me to appreciate the quality of the answer more than the form. Of course this didn't mean we didn't work on form; it just meant we didn't allow form to put on airs and assume greater importance than it deserved.

If the dinosaurs came back...
What would you do?
What would they do?

Steve's classmates went a little nuts when they saw his response. After a burst of admiration, someone said, "We have to do this again!" Imagine, third graders insisting that they be allowed to redo their homework. Be still, my heart. The second round produced these answers:

- If you were caught in a tree, you could jump on his neck and slide down.
- If you needed to cross a river, a bridgasaurus would be useful.
- If there were a fire and you were on the top floor, the dinosaur could rescue you.
- If the elevator in a skycraper got stuck, the dinosaur would rescue you.
- If you got stuck on a test, the dinosaur could stretch his neck over and see the answers to tell you.

I typed up all the homework responses and photocopied them for the group. When students read this second batch, they were thrilled by the word play of *bridgasaurus* and were eager to talk about other possibilities. "A watchasaurus could keep burglars away." "A slidasaurus would be good on the playground." The class said Mike Thaler and Ann Bishop and Peggy Parish would like these answers. They felt close to these authors because riddle books and Amelia Bedelia's zany misunderstandings had paved the path to reading for them. These children thought they hated reading until they found out you can play with words, twist meanings, and even make up your own words. Children had written to these authors and received replies, so it is no wonder they referred to authors as word fun colleagues, even as they did their homework.

Finally, I brought out the book *If the Dinosaurs Came Back*. Of course the children loved it and were amazed to find how closely some of their ideas resembled Bernard Most's. Then they began critiquing his work, decided his effort hadn't quite equaled their own *bridgasaurus*, *watchasaurus*, and *slidasaurus*. If Steve hadn't shown the way with his drawing and then Jesse with his *bridgasaurus*, the book would have produced delight but probably not discovery. What good luck that I didn't rush in with it. What good luck that I had established a tradition of sharing children's homework.* Children need time: time to return to an idea, time to try it again. They need time to learn to use humor just as much as they need time to learn the multiplication facts.

One of the joys of teaching is the way important issues resurface at unexpected moments. Months after we had dropped dinosaurs and moved on to other topics, Selene discovered *Who Wants a Cheap Rhinoceros?* She was excited to point out, "This is just like that dinosaur book!" A teacher knows she's doing something right when eight-year-olds understand that when the authors' intents are similar, the subject doesn't matter.

Valentine's Day brought us another echo of the dinosaur homework. I found a valentine card by Sandra Boynton with the friendly message, "Will you be my Valentinosaur?" When my students arrived at school they were greeted by a five-foot version of the card on our classroom door. They were jubilant. When I showed them the card that inspired this creation, they were impressed to learn that people earn their living making up wonderful words like *watchasaurus* and *valentinosaur.* Another thing that stunned my students is the fact that the Valentine card was for adults. Up until then they thought I was the only adult who enjoyed this kind of word play. Knowing that stores are filled with this kind of thing suddenly gave legitimacy to our vocabulary lessons.

Dinosaur word play had a last hurrah

*At least three times a week I typed up children's homework responses or classroom quick writes and sent them home with the assignment, "Read this aloud to an adult." The homework triumph came the day the custodian told me that the night before dads were reading aloud in a neighborhood bar a homework sheet on "advice for getting a hippopotamus stuck in the bathtub out." What a triumph when homework can reveal to dads just how clever and how funny their kids are. When children were absent, parents phoned to inquire if they'd missed "the good homework." If so, someone would drive to school to pick it up.

Read More

In *Happy Holidaysaurus!* Bernard Most offers additional linguistic possibilities. Underlying the kid-appealing silliness, the book delivers quite a lot of dinosaur lore, as well as information about how words work. Who said etymology has to be dull?

when I introduced hink-pinks. Steve proved once again that reading difficulties don't mean thinking difficulties by challenging his classmates with this one: "What's a huge dinosaur?" *Colossal fossil.*

In 1997, someone in Puffin marketing made a decision that reluctant readers and the adults who care about them should cheer for. They reissued Louis Phillips's *Wackysaurus Dinosaur Jokes* as part of the Puffin Chapters book series. Certainly this book is a legitimate chapter book; it has seven chapters. Chapter Four, "Waiter, There's a Dinosaur in My Soup!," gives a history of "something in my soup" riddle lore, showing readers that riddle makers stand on the shoulders of those who've gone before. Here are a few of the responses to the complaint of a dinosaur in the soup:

- Don't worry, sir, I'll take it back to the chef and exchange it for a fly.
- Don't yell so loudly. Everyone will want one.
- The chef ran out of flies.
- Don't worry. We don't charge extra.
- Don't worry. The soup's not hot enough to burn him.

    Why is there a dead dinosaur in my soup?
    The heat kills them.

And lots more. Such as the *Sauroscope*, a parody of the horoscope. Your birthday is on February 19? Then you are a *Piscescelarius*, destined to play tuba or trumpet, like the *protoceratops*, whose name means *first hornface.* The puns get even worse. A reluctant reader

Too Hot to Hoot: Funny Palindrome Riddles by Marvin Terban demonstrates that riddles depend on vocabulary clout. *Invisible Oink: Pig Jokes* by Louis Phillips has seven chapters of pig puns. One of the punch lines is Abra*ham* Lincoln. Another is *Hog*den Nash. A third is *Oink*le Sam. And a fourth is *Sow*san B. Anthony. Cultural literacy in high form!

who digs into this suddenly finds a reason for reading. So does his teacher.

Riddle Power

Never underestimate the power of riddle books. Steve entered third grade as a non-reader, a bright child who did his best to avoid books. Then one of his classmates read him a riddle from Joseph Heck's *Dinosaur Riddles*. "Read another one," Steve said. And he was hooked. For two months, Steve carried the

Teaching Tips

- Keep a supply of riddle books in a desk drawer. Offer extra credit for anybody who reads a riddle to you or to the class.

- Write a riddle on the board at the beginning of the day, challenging students to post possible answers. When you reveal the book answer at the end of the day, everybody may decide that some student answers are better.

- Reverse things. Give students the riddle answer and challenge them to come up with the question. Here are some answers from Marvin Terban's *Eight Ate: A Feast of Homonym Riddles*:

  a cheaper cheeper
  Aunt ant
  the nose knows
  a bizarre bazaar
  You hoo, you ewe!

Challenge students to come up with the questions.

- Giulio Maestro's riddles in *What's Mite Might? Homophone Riddles to Boost Your Word Power!* are more definitions than riddles, but Maestro has come up with homophone combinations that are vocabulary stretchers and that definitely have riddling possibilities. Challenge students to turn these into terrific riddles: *mite might, lynx links, jam jammed in a jamb, greater grater, grisly grizzly, airy aerie, idle idol, a quay key, a mean mien, frieze in a freeze, a vile vial.*

- Close out the day with riddle sessions. Encourage students to perfect their riddle-telling techniques: Stand and deliver.

- Encourage students to send a favorite riddle to people who make school and community life better, as a way of saying "thank you" for their services.

- Here's a list of words that have multiple meanings as nouns, which makes them easier to work with than noun-verb combinations. Invite students to write funny news headlines using these words. They can illustrate the headline. For example: *Car Jam Stalls Traffic* has definite possibilities.

band	bat	bed	block
brush	bulbs	bureau	can
coat	deck	gear	gift
glasses	horns	jam	legend
litter	log	palm	pen
pitcher	pool	rest	ring
scale	school	snap	title

Depending on your students' needs, you may want to give these out to aspiring humorists as a complete list or dole them out a few at a time.

book everywhere he went, working on making sense of its contents. Sometimes he asked me to tell him a word. Sometimes he said, "Listen to this one!" and read me a riddle. But mostly he just pored over that book, frowning, struggling, and, every once in a while, grinning. *Dinosaur Riddles* was the first book Steve ever read—and the second. As soon as he finished its 127 pages, Steve pronounced, "Best book I ever read." He stared at it for a moment and then turned to the first page. "I think I'll read it again." And he did.

Hink-Pinks

Sadly, Giulio Maestro's stupendous *Macho Nacho and Other Rhyming Riddles* is out of print (used copies are available at *Powells.com*, *Amazon.com*, and at *bn.com*). But don't let that stop you from sharing the concept of hink-pinks, hinky-pinkys, and other rhyming riddles. If you want to get technical, there are nine categories of hink-pinks, if you include homographs, homographs, and so on. But for our purposes, hink-pinks are one-syllable rhyming words; hinky-pinkys are two-syllable rhyming words; hinkety-pinketies are three-syllable rhyming words. The main reason to make the distinction is that signaling the number of syllables gives kids a hint as to the answer.

Here's a *hink-pink*:

How does an elephant take a shower?
With its nose hose.

Here's a *hinky-pinky*:

What do you call pasta for pooches?
Poodle noodles.

Ask your students the question for which *macho nacho* is the answer. Here's a *hinkety-pinkety*:

What do you call a monotonous (but not terrible) activity?
medium tedium

Bruce McMillan wrote two books of what he called terse verse—two-word poems that *Publishers Weekly* termed a "neat feat." *One Sun* and *Play Day* can be used as provocative answers to hink-pink riddles your students can create. What are the questions to which these word combinations are the answer?

bear chair
brown crown
fun run
lone stone
wet pet
stuck truck
pink drink

One nice thing about hink-pinks is that they move up the grades just by increasing the difficulty of the clues. Asking *What is an obese feline*, for example, asks for an easy answer (fat cat), but the clue words aren't so easy. Encourage students to search their social studies and science texts for words that lend themselves to this tomfoolery.

If students are studying, say, about the transcontinental railroad, then they should make a list of all the words that rhyme with *train*. Here are a few more answers:

Word Watch

Some people never outgrow hink-pinks. Here are some of the clues from the *New York Times* crossword puzzle from September 30, 1988:

de Gaulle description?
Humpty's big finish?
Barn dance?
Paging at an emporium?
Southern RSVP?

Answers: tall Gaul; wall fall; stall ball; mall call; y'all call

- George forge
- ready Teddy
- resident President
- rote vote

To make connections with science, try these answers:

- far star
- neat heat
- granite planet
- rotation location

Web Watch

Students can go to a rhyme site, such as *www.rhymezone.com,* put in a word, and get a list of possible combinations for hink-pink answers. Then all they have to do is come up with the questions.

Hink-pinks are a snap for some children but not for others. And you may be surprised by who ends up in which group. After spending several days in a second-grade classroom, at the end of my stay I decided to teach the children hink-pinks. Even the children who didn't catch on immediately were enthusiastic about this word play. Everybody got the answer when I told them that the answer to "rodent home" is "mouse house" or a "silly rabbit" is a "funny bunny," but some just could not come up with it on their own.

Teaching Tip

A good technique is to start children with simple one-syllable rhyming answers, asking them to supply the questions.

When a few parents stopped by after school, Camille and other students insisted that I teach *them* hink-pinks. Amazing to me, Camille's mother had exactly the same difficulty: She could get either the rhyming words or the synonyms for the right answer, but she could not put the two together. Maybe someone will read this and apply for a government grant to research the gene for hink-pinks.

I had been corresponding with these children all year, so I was quite familiar with them and their work. Based on what her teacher told me, what I'd seen of her written work, and my own observations over several days, Camille seemed to me to be the most verbally sophisticated of the group. She was such a terrific kid—smart, clever, generous, helpful. She was even terrifically well organized. At one point when her teacher and I were trying to get all the pieces in place for putting a complicated geography project in the school's display case, I said, "Let's put Camille in charge of checking that the posters of kids who think they're done have each required element." Not only did Camille handle this with ease, she gently told each one what additional element his poster needed. And if anybody needed help finding information in the encyclopedia, Camille was on the spot. What I admired was her understated manner. A lively, quick wit, she was not a showoff.

I was surprised when Camille was stumped by hink-pinks. Truly stumped. Her answers were either rhyming words or synonyms for the right answer, but she could not put rhyme and the synonym together. She didn't give up trying, but she never got it. Camille was a child who'd never known much "failure," and I was pleased that she faced this with such good spirits. The child who was quickest at hink-pinks was someone who struggled with reading.

A Literal Interpretation: Where an Eagle Eye Meets the Fork in the Road

Research shows us that readers who can make predictions while they read will also comprehend what they read. But if readers are to be predictors, they need to be interested and involved in what they read. Wacky books that rely on homonym mix-ups for their humor provide optimum conditions for high interest. Amelia Bedelia is, of course, the queen of misunderstanding homonyms and

TRY IT: Mixed-up Day

Directions

Write a to do list for the day. A few are done for you. Create illustrations for some of these expressions.

7 A.M.   Eat naval oranges.

8 A.M.   Run the vacuum cleaner.

9 A.M.   Join the car pool.

10 A.M.

11 A.M.   Work on putting a new wing on the house.

12 noon

1 P.M.

2 P.M.

3 P.M.

4 P.M.

5 P.M.

6 P.M.   Put china on the table.

7 P.M.

8 P.M.   Paint the town red.

9 P.M.   Hit the hay.

taking things literally. Told to draw the drapes when the sun comes in, Amelia dutifully sits down with a sketchpad. Young readers who groan, "Oh, no!" when Amelia is told to "plant the bulbs" or "check the shirts" are well on their way to reading power. They are recognizing multiple meanings, reading for detail, drawing inferences, anticipating outcomes. Most important, they are loving reading. Increasing their vocabulary is a nice bonus.

In *Max's Wacky Taxi Day*, Max Grover mines verbal and visual possibilities when Max the taxi driver encounters the literal interpretation of such expressions as *spring showers, airplane hangar, socked in by fog, a tooth ferry, a car phone, a fork in the road, a traffic jam,* and *a rock concert*. The phrases carried to their literal absurdities in the artwork are printed in bold red letters in the text, of special help to beginning punsters and second language users. Max and his taxi are in the grand tradition established by Amelia and followed by Fred Gwynne in his hilarious series of zany titles based on homonym mix-ups.

In a Pickle and Other Idioms

Idioms are a rich source of word play. How would Amelia Bedelia interpret "I smell a rat?" Even though this idiom has been around since 1550 or so, Amelia, being probably the most literal, concrete thinker on the planet, will call the exterminator. But for the rest of us idioms have become codes, a lan-

Read More

Marvin Terban's *In a Pickle and Other Funny Idioms, Punching the Clock: Funny Action Idioms,* and *Mad as a Wet Hen!* are three books that have stood the test of time. Terban's *Scholastic Dictionary of Idioms* is a good, kid-friendly reference book. If your school library doesn't have *The American Heritage Dictionary of Idioms* by Christine Ammer, ask them to get it.

Read More

For adult readers: *Idiom's Delight* by Suzanne Brock offers fascinating phrases in Spanish, French, Italian, and Latin. We say "Go fly a kite!" in English; in Spanish, they say "Go fry asparagus!" and in French, "Go cook an egg!" Sadly, this entertaining and erudite volume is out of print, but it's worth looking for.

Idiom Savant: Slang as It Is Slung by Jerry Dunn offers an exhaustive list of the colorful lingo of American subcultures, from Animators to Zine readers. Here we get the slang of wildly different groups, from bird watchers to magicians, FBI agents, firefighters, sky divers, restaurant workers, wrestlers, and lots more.

In *When a Loose Cannon Flogs a Dead Horse There's the Devil to Pay*, Olivia A. Isil offers a compendium of seafaring words in everyday speech. Did you know *hunky-dory*, meaning "A-OK," probably had its origins in Honkidori, a street in Yokohama, Japan? Or that *bonanza* is derived from the Spanish *bonanza*, meaning *to sail with fair wind and weather*? This book will provide you with a way to delight and inform your students with a story a day for many days. Similarly, Robert Hendrickson's *QPB Encyclopedia of Word and Phrase Origins* is a goldmine of stories about words.

guage within a language. Because the meaning of an idiom cannot be deduced from the definitions of each word, idioms mystify outsiders. Idioms also intensify the feelings of kinship among members of the tribe who use them. Idioms don't travel well to other languages. This is why a rich baby, born with a silver spoon in his mouth in the U.S., is born in France with a hat and in Italy arrives wearing a shirt.

Riddles from Idioms

The word idiom comes from *idios*, meaning *own, personal, private*. Because an idiom is an expression of a given language that is peculiar to itself, it works particularly well in humor. In one sense, the more an expression is peculiar to a given people, the funnier the

Check Your Idioms

Directions

See if you know the meanings of these idioms. Write what each means.

1. Bark up the wrong tree.

2. You can bet your boots.

3. Pass the buck.

4. Hold your horses.

5. Keep up with the Joneses.

6. That's for the birds.

7. He's all wet.

8. to be called on the carpet

9. to burn one's bridges

10. Cut corners.

11. If the shoe fits . . .

12. Paint the town red.

What Do You Do When You're in a Pickle?

We use idioms all the time, without even thinking about what the literal meaning of the expression would be.

Directions
Create fun illustrations for a few of these idioms. A person who:

- is cracking up
- has lost his mind
- is willing to give a friend a hand
- stands head and shoulders above the rest
- has a green thumb
- is in a pickle
- is seeing red
- is under the weather
- is punching a time clock

Think of some other phrases that would be fun to illustrate.

Word-Within-a-Word Riddles

What is the feline's favorite book?
*A cat*alogue.

Challenge
Make some riddles out of these cat words. You will need a dictionary. Lots of these words are difficult and have very special meanings. **Note:** Some words that begin with *cat*—such as *cathedral*—are not on this list because you don't say the *cat* in the word the way you say it in *cat*. For the joke to work, the *cat* has to be pronounced the same.

catastrophe	cataclysm
cataract	catsup
category	catacomb
catalyst	catbird
catfish	caterpillar
catgut	catwalk
cat-o'-nine-tails	catnap
cattle	cattail
cat's cradle	catty corner
catamaran	catatonia
CAT scan	raining cats and dogs

joke seems. If you get the joke, you are a member of the select group. Idioms, then, offer children a unique way to play with words. But to play, they have to do the hard work of first getting the idiom. This set of activities, based on idioms, is designed to help children experience that wonderful moment of discovery, of making a particular language expression their own and creating something new with that language. The idiomatic puzzles start easy and get increasingly difficult. You may be surprised by who can and cannot get visual puzzles, such as Wordograms (see pages 105–107). One of the nice things is that such puzzles often allow divergent thinkers, who might not do well on typical literacy fare, to shine.

The Fractured Facts (see pages 108–109) work with idioms can be a way to get your students hooked on history. When students get a riddle such as "Why did Benjamin Franklin make the first eyeglasses? *Because he wanted to make a spectacle of himself*," they're demonstrating both historical savvy and familiarity with the multiple meanings of words.

Here are some guidelines you can give fledgling riddling historians:

1. Choose a famous person and read a biography of that person.
2. List some important events and deeds in that person's life.
3. Check the list for homonyms, words with more than one meaning.
4. Check the list for words that are contained in common idioms (*kite*, for example).

5. Be aware of synonyms (*eyeglasses* and *spectacles*, for example).
6. Keep a list of common idioms handy. After reading the biography, see if any of those idioms might be a punch line to a riddle.
7. Let an idiom-based riddle substitute for a book report.

Combining Words for New Creations

In *Supposes* (out of print but available used from online bookstores, though you can use his technique without his book), Dick Gackenbach helps children see words in new ways, employing verbal antics to encourage children to engage in word play.

- Suppose a cat ate lemons. *Then she'd be a sourpuss!*
- Suppose a rabbit was a table. *Then you would eat a hamburger on a bunny!*

Gackenbach's approach not only encourages word fun, it also provides one more way to look at idiomatic expressions.

Both James Howe and Norman Juster make creative use of combination word play, combining two words to make a new word. For example, James Howe's *Bunnicula* is the combination of *bunny* and *Dracula*. In *The Phantom Tollbooth*, one of the combination words Norman Juster creates is *dictionopolis*. Douglas Florian titled one of his books *Laugh-eteria*. This *-eteria* combination offers lots of possibilities for children. For starters, what *-eterias* would they like to see installed in the school?

Sometimes life imitates art. The Chunnel, which permits passengers to ride in a high-speed train across the English Channel between England and France, is a combination of *tunnel* and *channel*.

Combining Words (on pages 110–111) provide a series of activities encouraging students to try this technique.

Body Builders

Directions

Think of as many idioms as you can that describe parts of the body. There are some here to help you get started. The lines under an expression mean you should find more idioms in that category. For example, under *cross your fingers,* you might put *green thumb.*

eyes in the back of his head

_____

_____

_____

hair standing on end

_____

_____

_____

pea-brained

_____

_____

_____

pay through the nose

_____

_____

_____

wet behind the ears

_____

_____

_____

all thumbs

_____

_____

_____

cat's got his tongue

_____

_____

_____

pain in the neck

_____

_____

_____

heart in right place

_____

_____

_____

Cartoon Connections I

Directions

Choose one or more of the idioms below. Write a definition of what it means. Then draw a picture that shows what Amelia Bedelia might think it means. For example, *I'm on a roll* might show someone sitting on top of a huge cinnamon bun.

She's all washed up.

He likes to throw his weight around.

She's on the mend.

He drives me up a tree.

They gave him the third degree.

I guess I'll have to eat crow.

Don't let the cat out of the bag.

Her eyes are bigger than her stomach.

Cartoon Connections II

Directions

Choose one or more of the idioms below. Write a definition of what it means. Then draw a picture that shows what Amelia Bedelia might think it means. For example, *You'd better shake a leg* might show a man vigorously shaking one of his legs.

She didn't bat an eye.

She studied around the clock.

Let's shoot the breeze.

He beat me to the punch.

That book gave me goose bumps.

He's a chain smoker.

I'd like to give you a piece of my mind.

He gave me the cold shoulder.

Cut out the horseplay.

Don't pull my chain.

Wordograms I

Directions

Look at these pictures very carefully. Try to discover a familiar saying in each of them.
Hint: Notice the way the letters of words are placed in the boxes. Notice whether one word is above another word, or to the right or left. These things can be important clues.

1. wink wink wink wink wink wink wink wink
   wink wink wink wink wink wink wink wink
   wink wink wink wink wink wink wink wink
   wink wink wink wink wink wink wink wink
   wink wink wink wink wink wink wink wink

2. BEND
   BEND (inverted)

3. CALL

4. thing thing

5. B B A T
   BUSH A
   T A

6. All
   but the shouting

7. ObNE'S BONeNeET

8. M   M
   A   P

9. **HORSE**

10. ever
    ever   ever
    ever
    ever

© 2002 by Susan Ohanian from *The Great Word Catalogue: FUNdamental Activities for Building Vocabulary*. Portsmouth, NH: Heinemann.

Wordograms II

Directions
Look at these pictures very carefully. Try to discover a familiar saying in each of them.
Hint: Notice the way the letters of words are placed in the boxes. Notice whether one word is above another word, or to the right or left. These things can be important clues

1. Think Think	**2.** EARTH FOOT FOOT
3. sitting earth	**4.** ME A L
5. PUPIL LENS CORNEA BELLY	**6.** Wether
7. Quack Peep Cock-a-doodle-doo Gobble	**8.** I'm Myself
9. ICE	**10.** KNOCK maple oak pine

' 2002 by Susan Ohanian from *The Great Word Catalogue: FUNdamental Activities for Building Vocabulary*. Portsmouth, NH: Heinemann.

Wordograms III

Directions

Look at these pictures very carefully. Try to discover a familiar saying in each of them.
Hint: Notice the way the letters of words are placed in the boxes. Notice whether one word is above another word, or to the right or left. These things can be important clues.

1.
IT
e
c
a
f

2.
F
A
C
E

3.
year year year year year year year year year year
year year year year year year year year year year
year year year year year year year year year year
year year year year year year year year year year
year year year year year year year year year year
year year year year never year year year year year
year year year year year year year year year year
year year year year year year year year year year
year year year year year year year year year year
year year year year year year year year year year
year year year year year year year year year year

4.
Tricorn
Coonskin cap
Fedora

5.
D
E
F

6.
P
I
P
E

7.
Smart   Bright
Intelligent Clever

8.
Walking
atmosphere

9.
PRICE

10.
feline
ice

Fractured Facts I

Directions

Match each idiom with one of the historical people listed at the bottom of the page. **Hint:** There should be a clue in the idiom that tells something about what the historical person did. Once you have a match, then see if you can turn it into a riddle. The first one is done for you.

1. Go fly a kite! _a_
   What did Benjamin Franklin's brother say to him when Benjamin was being a pest?

2. Why don't you paddle your own canoe? ____

3. I'm looking for a ballpark figure. ____

4. I had a whale of a time. ____

5. He just needs to let off steam. ____

6. There's no use crying over spilled milk. ____

7. Let's look at where the rubber meets the road. ____

8. That's not my cup of tea. ____

9. He's the apple of my eye. ____

10. YOUR TURN. Try to invent a historical riddle.

a. Benjamin Franklin's brother
b. John Chapman's mother
c. Herman Melville
d. Gail Borden
e. Samuel Adams
f. Babe Ruth's wife
g. Sacagawea
h. Robert Fulton's wife
i. Charles Goodyear

© 2002 by Susan Ohanian from *The Great Word Catalogue: FUNdamental Activities for Building Vocabulary*. Portsmouth, NH: Heinemann.

Fractured Facts II

Directions

Match each idiom with one of the historical people listed at the bottom of the page. **Hint:** There should be a clue in the idiom that tells something about what the historical person did. Once you have a match, then see if you can turn it into a riddle.

1. Quit horsing around. _____

2. I'll take you for a ride. _____

3. Boys will be boys. _____

4. You light up my life. _____

5. He gave me a cold shoulder. _____

6. Don't tell me to stick to my knitting! _____

7. Toot your own horn. _____

8. Don't be a penny pincher. _____

9. He just wants to make a spectacle of himself. _____

10. YOUR TURN. Try to invent a historical riddle. _____

a. Abraham Lincoln
b. Thomas Edison's wife
c. Paul Revere's wife
d. Henry Ford
e. Betsy Ross
f. Jesse James's mother
g. John Philip Sousa
h. Clarence Birdseye
i. Benjamin Franklin

© 2002 by Susan Ohanian from *The Great Word Catalogue: FUNdamental Activities for Building Vocabulary*. Portsmouth, NH: Heinemann.

Combining Words

Dick Gackenbach once invented a game called *Supposes*.

■ Suppose a cat ate lemons. *Then she would be a sourpuss!*
■ Suppose a rabbit was a table. *Then you would eat a hamburger on a bunny!*

Now it's your turn. Try writing your own *supposes*. **Hint:** it's easier to start with *then*. Try writing a *Suppose* statement to go with these *Then* statements.

1. Suppose _____. Then he'd be a doorman.

2. Suppose _____. Then you'd have a dragonfly.

3. Suppose _____. Then it would be doggone.

Now try making up the whole item for these words: *ballroom, carpet, horseradish, houseplant, houseplant, kingpin,* and *mushroom.*

Student: Combining Words

In *The Amazing Frecktacle* by Ross Venokur combines *freckles* with *spectacle* to get *frecktacle*. Your task is to think of some words that could be combined with that *-tacle* ending to mean *a real display of something, good or bad*.

Try the same thing with *spectacular*, which is even more impressive than a spectacle.

Word combinations are all around us. For example, *Amtrak* is a word created from combining *American tracks*; *motel* comes from *motorist's hotel*. What words do you think are combined to make *infomercial*?

Your Turn
- Look around for more combined words. You can look for them in the supermarket, on TV, on billboards, and in lots of other places.
- Invent some combined words. For example, what two things at school could you combine to invent a new term?

Foods offer interesting possibilities for combining words. For example, Tex/Mex is food that combines flavors of Texas and Mexico. Invent a menu for food combinations you create. You can combine cities, states, or countries. Or maybe you'll think of something else to combine.

Animal Antics

Poet J. Patrick Lewis writes about what a *hippopotamusn't* and what a *hippopotamust.* And Lewis calls a rhino who told lies of incredible size *Rhinocchio.*

1. Can you think of some different endings for a hippopotamus or a rhinoceros?
2. How about an elephant? Laura Richards wrote a famous poem about the elephant who tried to use the *telephant.* Or was it the *elephone* using the *telephone?* Can you think of any other animal entanglements?
3. Consider the *pelican* and the *pelican't.* And the *centipedestrian.*

It's Eelementary

Poet Douglas Florian writes that eels are smart—because *they go to eelementary school.* Think of some other *eely* words. For help, you can check out words beginning with *el* in the dictionary. Add an extra *e* and you have an *eely* word. Make a list of *eely* words and then write a riddle or a poem using some of these words.

Food for Thought

In his poem "Turnips Turn Up" Douglas Florian writes that "Turnips turnup in salad bowls." Florian is an expert in word combining: He says the salty sea makes the walrus "walrusty"; that the baby kangaroo is fast asleep "inside its kangaroom"; that a rhea is "an ostrich rhearranged."

In *Oodles of Noodles,* Lucia and James L. Hymes, Jr. write, "Noodles are my favorite foodles." In "Italian Noodles," X. J. Kennedy doesn't combine words but he changes the spelling when he describes eating ravioli:

I fork it quick
but chew it sloli.

Your Turn
Make a list of foods. Then try to invent combinations and spellings to go with them.

Crocosilly

Poets love to play with words. Look at what Joan Bransfield Graham writes in "Crocodile Tears":

Oh, crocodile poor crocodillo
cried so hard you soaked your pillow.

1. Think of what you would call a crocodile who eats taffy or jelly.
2. Write some other two-line poems involving a crocodile. As a poet, you can change its name any way you want.
3. Write a riddle involving a crocodile. Here's a sample:

What happened to the crocodile who ate two tons of jelly?
He ended up with a croco-belly.

ABCs with a Difference

Alphabet books should be moved up from the preschool shelves to middle grades. The good ones offer lots of possibility for creative word play and vocabulary stretching. But if you think the picture book format will turn older kids off—or if you don't have these particular books—then take the idea to your students.

■ The Caldecott Medal book *Ashanti to Zulu: African Traditions* by Margaret Musgrove offers insights about twenty-six African tribes and provides a model for students to create their own display of what they know of the words, customs, habits, and general culture of a people they are studying. Whether it's colonial New England or ancient Greece or South America, the creation of a cultural ABC book is both challenging and informative.

■ Marcia Brown's *Peter Piper's Alphabet* is a golden oldie, but the verses were taken from the much older *Peter Piper's Practical Principles of Plain and Perfect Pronunciation*, first published in London in 1813. Children, of course, find such tongue twisters irresistible. But a real shock is in store for them if you give a homework assignment along the lines of *Who is the oldest person you can find who knows Peter Piper?* Children are

amazed to discover that their parents and *their* parents and *their* parents are very familiar with this old favorite. The challenge then is for kids to create an alphabet of tongue twisters, both borrowed and original. One way to do this is to let everyone choose an alphabet letter out of a hat and send them home with the assignment of writing a tongue twister starring that letter. Then, type up all the contributions and send home the class anthology with the challenge: *Read this to a friend. Ask the friend to read it to you.*

■ Leonard E. Fisher's *Alphabet Art* is out of print but well worth tracking down in a library. It is a treasure trove of sumptuous art and information. Fisher gives us thirteen alphabets in use around the world today: Arabic, Cherokee, Chinese, Cyrillic, Eskimo, Gaelic, German, Greek, Hebrew, Japanese, Sanskrit, Thai, and Tibetan. This book is an across-the-curriculum inspiration all by itself, combining art, language, history, and culture.

■ Is there a child alive who hasn't doodled an ABC list of names? Students are enchanted to see such a list turned into a book. In Karen Ackerman's *Flannery Row: An Alphabet Rhyme* Commander Ahab Flannery says good-bye to his 26 children—Ahab through Zack. In *Nonsense! He Yelled*, Roger Eschbacher offers silly rhymes with an alphabet of boys' names, and on the last page he offers the challenge,

> Good-bye! Good-bye!
> We say good-bye.
> It's sad we're out of time.
> Before we go,
> won't **you** please try
> Your **own name** in a rhyme?

Invite students to accept the challenge.

■ Alphabet books don't have to be sweetness and light. Invite students to provide derogatory descriptors to go with alphabetic names: *abominable Alex, bullying Betsy*. Or they can pair them up with noisy verbs: *Anna argues, Bobby belches*. Or ways of moving: *Archy ambles, Barbara bounces*. Provide a safety net by decreeing that no name of anyone in the class may be used.

■ You can require an adjective, noun, verb, and direct object or object of a preposition, all beginning with the same letter:

> Agile antelope appeal for apples.
> Bristly bears burrow for berries.

Remind students that this isn't just a rote exercise of plugging in parts of speech. They should do some research, finding adjectives that make sense (or superb and sly nonsense) with the nouns. Tell them that in *Alfred's Alphabet Walk*, Victoria Chess describes alligators as *ancient*. Could there be a better adjective for those creatures?

■ Anita Lobel is a master of the alphabet genre. Her *Alison's Zinnia* established a model for the circular pattern format, starting with *Alison acquired an Amaryllis for Beryl* and ending with *Zena zeroed in on a Zinnia for Alison*. There's beautiful art, magical flower names, and intriguing verbs. A note at the end tells the reader that Lobel was inspired by the alphabetic street names she encountered on a visit to Vero Beach, Florida, making students aware that vivacious vocabulary is all around us.

■ *Away from Home* is another masterful alphabet pattern book by Anita Lobel. This time, boys' names are featured as well as foreign locations, from *Adam arriving in Amsterdam* to *Zachary zigzagging in Zaandam*. Children get a geographic lesson as well as vocabulary that's out of the ordinary.

■ In Nicholas Heller's *Goblins in Green*, stylish goblins get all dressed up, from *Annabelle is attired in an amber blouse* through *Zelda, zipped in her zebra anorak*. Curiously, *Bedford is wearing bright blue chinos*. One can only wonder about this lapse in the pattern, the only lapse among the twenty-six entries. Challenging students to find an appropriate substitute for *wearing* will set them on quite a vocabulary search.

■ Heller uses the same pattern in *Ogres! Ogres! Ogres!* which has the subtitle *A Feasting Frenzy from A to Z*. He doesn't mess this one up—from *Abednego adores anchovy butter* to *Zuleika zips zealously through her asparagus!* it is a culinary and vocabulary delight. Note the progression that ends up, like Lobel's *Alison's Zinna*, being circular. In between there is quite a feast, including *Una upends urns of vichyssoise* and *Voracious Vlad vanquishes the watermelons*. Children can enjoy the books without knowing the meaning of *zealously, vichyssoise, voracious,* and *vanquishes*. But it's these encounters with wonderfully mysterious words that make vocabularies grow.

■ Numerous alphabet books employ a name and food theme. Anne Shelby's *Potluck* employs a simpler vocabulary: *Ben brought bagels, Edmund entered with enchiladas,* and so on. Crescent Dragonwagon's *Alligator Arrives with Apples* describes an unusual alphabetic Thanksgiving meal. Rex Barron's *Fed Up! A Feast of Frazzled Foods* offers alphabetic foods with an edge: *Hot dog Hates Hot sauce, Impatient Ice cream . . . Melon Melee, Nauseated Nectarine*. In *Alphabet Soup*, Abbie Zabar offers playful word stories about food, and what each food is. From *antipasto, borscht,* and *couscous* to *x-ray fish, Yorkshire pudding,* and *zabaglione*, Zabar offers food from around the world.

Web Watch

This website has the sounds of animals around the world: *www.georgetown.edu/cball/animals/animals.html*. Students can find out not everybody thinks frogs say "Ribbit."

Afrikaans: kwaak-kwaak
Arabic (Algeria): gar gar
Catalan: cruá-cruá
Croatian: kre-kre
Dutch: kwak kwak
English (GB): croak
Finnish: kvak kvak
German: quaak, quaak
Hebrew: kwa kwa (/qva qva)
Hungarian: bre-ke-ke
Japanese: kerokero
Norwegian: kvekk-kvekk
Russian: kva-kva
Spanish (Argentina): berp
Swedish: kvack
Turkish: vrak vrak

Albanian: kuak kuak
Bengali: gangor-gangor
Chinese (Mandarin): guo guo
Danish: kvæk
English (U.S.A.): ribbit
Estonian: krooks-krooks
French: coa-coa
Greek (Ancient Greek): brekekekex koax koax
Hindi: me:ko:me:k-me:ko:me:k
Italian: cra cra
Korean: gae-gool-gae-gool
Polish: kum kum
Spanish (Spain): cruá-cruá
Spanish (Peru): croac, croac
Thai: ob ob (with high tone)
Ukrainian: kwa-kwa

■ Speaking of vocabulary growth, Jeanne and William Steig's *Alpha Beta Chowder* offers an alphabet of wacky verses and will challenge and delight, from verses about an *abhorent axolotl*, a *bellicose brigand*, and *gruesome Gilbert* to *noisome Naomi*, whose parents are nitwits, and Vera who might have been downed by a vampire's venom, and so on, including ecology and endangered and extinct animals. Miska Miles's *Apricot ABC* presents a complete science lesson, revealing an ecological mystery within an alphabetic structure. Busy bees and crawling caterpillars inhabit the meadow, but there is also a villain, a crisis, and a resolution. Norma's Farber's classic *As I Was Crossing Boston Common* pictures mysterious, beguiling animals from *angwantibo* to *zibet*, with notes at the end. Patricia Mullins's *V for Vanishing: An Alphabet of Endangered Animals* is presented in the style of the traditional alphabet book for the youngest set: One word and one picture per page, with the name of the specific species and the scientific name added, giving young readers an introduction to etymology.

Dd Dolphin
Indus River Dolphin
Platanista indi
Pakistan

Look closely and you see that Mullins has included animals from every continent except Antarctica. So the child who is drawn in by beautiful pictures of animals gets a lesson in etymology and geography as well. This is what good alphabet books do—deliver more than first meets the eye.

■ Ann Jonas's *Aardvarks, Disembark!* will captivate the youngest readers (even if they can't pronounce the names *addaxes* through *zorils*). The unique organization of this book makes it a breathtaking, sobering tour de force; it concludes with a list of the 132 species of animals pictured in the book.

■ Ron Wilson's *100 Dinosaurs from A to Z* is neither clever or beautiful, but in its straightforward presentation of dinosaur facts, it provides a model for young writers trying to organize nonfiction information.

■ *Annie, Bea, and Chi Chi Dolores: A School*

Day Alphabet by Donna Mauer looks very simple. With pictures by Denys Cazet, and one word or simple phrase per page, it would be a hard sell above first or second grade. But you can take the concept to older students. *Counting, drawing, erasing . . .* each page describes what young children do in a school day. What a challenge for older kids! Can they describe their day alphabetically?

■ Alan Snow's *The Monster Book of ABC Sounds* is unique. Delivering on its title, it offers an alphabet of sounds. The monsters are unremarkable but the sounds are great, from *Aaah! Boo! Cooeee!* to *Vrroom! Wheeeeee* and so on. This is a case where it's better *not* to show the book before introducing the idea to students. This one's out of print, but after students try their hand at alphabet noises, show them Bobbi Katz's *Rumpus of Rhymes: A Book of Noisy Poems.* They will be wowed by her noises.

■ In *Gathering the Sun,* Alma Flor Ada offers an alphabet of poems in Spanish and English: *arboles/trees* to *zanahoria/carrot.* Lynn Rowe Reed's *Pedro, His Perro, and the Alphabet Sombrero* offers a simple alphabetic list of Spanish words, but the vibrant cubist-quality illustrations add sophistication that may convince older readers that there's something for them. A note at the end translates the Spanish, offers a little etymology, and explains why there is no *w* word. Again, if the book is not available, take the concept: What items from A to Z can you hang on a sombrero, or on a hat from another land?

Stephanie Poulin's *Ah! Belle Cité!* offers an alphabetic look at a city in French and English. James Rice's *Cajun Alphabet* is an introduction to the patois of l'arcady French of Louisiana. Again, you don't need these specific titles. Take the premise of exploring a culture through an ABC structure in the language of the student's choice.

Patricia Borlenghi's *From Albatross to Zoo* offers other possibilities. It alphabetically presents animals in five languages and we learn that *zoo* is the same in German, French, Spanish, and Italian. Offer collaboration possibilities to students of different language backgrounds. What subject will they choose: animal, mineral, or vegetable? How about furniture? Clothing? Sports?

■ *Eight Hands Round: A Patchwork Alphabet* by Ann Whitford Paul describes twenty-six different quilt patterns and gives their historical contexts. It is an intriguing premise to take an artifact and through it present information about a people. Michael McCurdy's *The Sailor's Alphabet* is also historical, offering students a tour of a United States Navy frigate from the 1800s, from the anchor and bowsprit to stilliards and topsails, though McCurdy has to say "uncle" on X and Z.

■ An alphabet book can be a format for students presenting words from their vocabulary journals and an inspiration to find more. Jeanne Jeffares's *An Around-the-World Alphabet Book* offers both conventional and unusual words:

D is for ding-dong bells, dunce, dromedary, dianthus.

In *Comic and Curious Cats,* Angela Carter offers love poems to cats:

I love my cat with an E
Although she is Elephantine
Epicurean
And Edacious
Her name is Emilia
She lives in Edgware
And she eats Everything Earnestly.

Anybody who thinks alphabet books are for babies can try his hand at this structure: three adjectives, a place name, two adverbs, all with the same letter.

■ Alphabet books can be puzzles. A sophisticated concept about process and creation belies the simple appearance of George Shannon's *Tomorrow's Alphabet.*

A is for seed—tomorrow's apple.
B is for eggs—tomorrow's birds.

Mary Elting's classic *Q Is for Duck: An Alphabet Guessing Game* has entertained readers for almost two decades. There's a good reason it has not gone out of print. Once readers see just one puzzle answer, they are hooked. It is a challenging model for emulation. If you don't have the book, just offer students the premise: *Q is for Duck because . . . Ducks quack.*

In *Easy as Pie*, Marcia and Michael Folsom offer an alphabetic guessing game of simple idioms. The fact that the alphabet letter is the first letter of the answer makes finding the missing part of the idiom a snap. *Cool as a Cucumber, Dark as a Dungeon*, and so on. The book is out of print, but the model it provides is available: Put the idiom on one page, leaving off the last word. The first letter of the last

Student: Word Watch

Animals Eating

Consider writing a rhyming ABC of animals bringing food to a party: *Antelopes bring cantelopes. Bears bring éclairs.* Now that the animal food fest is started, can you finish it?

You can make your task more challenging by making the animals, verb, and food all start with the same letter: *Antelopes arrive with artichokes. Bears bring bananas.* And so on.

For a super challenge, include a geographic place in your alphabetic list.

Antelopes arrive in Amsterdam with artichokes. Bears bring bananas to Boston.

This challenge can expand as much as you want. Here's what happens when you add adjectives and adverbs:

Amiable antelopes avidly accept artichokes in attractive Amsterdam.
Boisterous bears belatedly bring banana bunches to breezy Boston.

A number of writers and artists have created alphabet books about the places in which they live, urban and rural. Look around and see how many A to Z things are in your life. Write a book!

Here's an idea for a different sort of alphabet book. Try using letters two at a time. Here are some combinations from Angela Carter's *Comic and Curious Cats*: *They are beautiful and capricious; they eat begonias and carnations.*

What could you say about cats (or dogs) using two consecutive letters of the alphabet?

Choose a subject for an alphabet book and try describing it two letters at a time. Angela Carter let *A* stand alone. You can do that too, or you can start your book by using *A* and *B* together, then *C* and *D*, and so on.

Writers are always looking for ways to make their work a little different. When Fritz Eichenberg wrote *Ape in a Cape*, he presented animals from A to Z, and he gave each animal a rhyme: *Owl on the prowl; pig in a wig.* It is clear that Fritz Eichenberg was looking for rhymes that would allow him to draw amusing pictures to illustrate them. You don't need to see this book to try the same idea.

My Day from A to Z

Directions

Try making up an alphabetic schedule for a busy day. You might start out with *asleep* or *bed-making*. Can you keep it going? Exaggeration and fantasy are allowed. You may decide to make someone else's schedule, such as a fairy tale character, an athlete, an astronaut, or a firefighter. Your choice.

My Day from A to Z

6:00 A.M.	3:00 P.M.
7:00 A.M.	3:30 P.M.
8:00 A.M.	4:00 P.M.
9:00 A.M.	4:30 P.M.
10:00 A.M.	5:00 P.M.
10:30 A.M.	5:30 P.M.
11:00 A.M.	6:00 P.M.
11:30 A.M.	7:00 P.M.
12:00 noon	7:30 P.M.
1:00 P.M.	8:00 P.M.
1:30 P.M.	9:00 P.M.
2:00 P.M.	10:00 P.M.
2:30 P.M.	12 midnight

Super Alphabetic Challenge

How many words would you need to have to use all the letters of the alphabet? What's the least number of letters you need to use in order to have all twenty-six letters?

Something to think about: Find five words that use only letters in the first half of the alphabet. Find five words that use only the second half of the alphabet. Which list do you think will be easier? Why?

Word Watch

In 1842, this ad appeared in *The Times*.

WANTED: Situation to superintend the household and preside at table. The lady is Agreeable, Becoming, Careful, Desirable, English, Facetious, Generous, Honest, Industrious, Judicious, Keen, Likely, Merry, Natty, Obedient, Philosophic, Quiet, Regular, Sociable, Tasteful, Useful, Womanish, Xantippish, Youthful, Zealous, and etc.

Challenge: Ask students to write their own alphabetic ad seeking employment. Ask them to write an alphabetic list of what qualities they desire in a friend.

word tells you where to place the idiom in an alphabetic collection. This structure works well for creating pop-up puzzlers.

Michael Roberts's *The Jungle ABC* also presents a puzzle, but you have to see this one. Best known for his *New Yorker* collage covers, Roberts presents a spectacular oversized collage ABC, and except for the puzzle solutions at the end, it is wordless. Once you see it, you will understand how a wordless book finds its way into a book about growing vocabulary.

More alphabetic puzzles are offered in two elegant volumes by Cathi Hepworth: *Antics!* and *Bug Off!* Hepworth invites students to find the pesky little words inside much larger words. Richard Wilbur's *The Disappearing Alphabet* does the opposite, offering twenty-six poetic examples of what happens when letters started disappearing

from words. Either way, these books set readers to thinking about the way words are made as well as what they mean.

For students who still insist that alphabet books are too tame, hand them Michael Roberts's *Mumbo Jumbo: The Creepy ABC*. Lavish art combines with macabre verses. The short verses are sly and sophisticated, the images spooky. This book is for older kids.

Creating an alphabet book can be a way of organizing a universe of information. There are alphabet books about airports, firefighters, Native Americans, African animals, frogs, wildflowers, architecture, farmers, caribou, trees, railroads, astronauts, extinct animals, food, ocean life, deserts, insects, and snakes. The content can be simple or complex, the delivery straightforward or zany. Tim Arnold's *Natural History from A to Z* and Max Grover's *The Accidental Zucchini*, for example, are a study in contrasts. From the anteater to the zebra, Arnold's book offers informative descriptions of habitat, physical characteristics, and habits of animals and plants in many parts of the world, with each animal and plant demonstrating an important biological concept. Grover's offbeat offering delivers on his subtitle: *An Unexpected Alphabet*, offering apple autos, bathtub boat, and cupcake canyon through zigzag zoo. The reader is transported into a world of magic realism, with each illustration actually picturing each unlike word combo. You'd never thought of octopus overalls before? Look at this book and you'll see that they are possible.

Some alphabet books are breathtaking in concept and delivery, helping us look at language relationships in new ways. The ABCs are a good structure in which to encourage children to strive for excellence, searching for just the right word to fit a pattern. The activities provided are designed so that every child can contribute and some are prodded to stretch further.

Palindromes

According to an old joke, Adam's first words to Eve were, "Madam, I'm Adam." *Palindromes:* You either love them or scorn them. Will Shortz, *New York Times* Crossword Editor and National Public Radio "Puzzle-master," says that *I Love Me, Vol. I* by Michael Donner "is either the largest, most thoroughly researched, and most entertainingly annotated collection of palindromes ever compiled or else the ramblings of a disturbed mind. I haven't decided which." Donner offers 3,500 palindromes with amusing and informative commentaries throughout. Open the book at random and you'll soon be hooked:

> *eel glee:* Electric merriment.
>
> *U Nu:* Former premier of Burma, 1950s and early 1960s.
>
> *UNU:* United Nations University
>
> *UN U Nu:* The Burmese premier when he was associated with the United Nations, and when he is associated with United Nations University he is *UNU U Nu.*

The book also lists signal palindromic years with Donner's unique take on historical events that occurred.

The endpapers to Jon Agee's *Go Hang a Salami, I'm a Lasagna Hog!* provide a ready-made introductory lesson on palindromes. Both this and Agee's other palindromic offering, *So Many Dynamos!*, have palindromic ISBNs—and cover prices ($12.21). What's more, the first book was published in 1991

and is dedicated to Hannah. The art is a huge part of the fun in these books. Agee provides a street scene with palindromes that make perfect sense in the scene: *noon, nun, eve, Bob, eye.* Palindromes grow more complex, with the art provoking one to do a double take on the language: *Tahiti hat, wonton? Not now, salt an atlas, llama mall, stack cats,* and lots more.

Variations on a Theme

There are lots of wonderful versions of old favorites like *The House That Jack Built* and *I Know an Old Lady Who Swallowed a Fly.* Books that change the traditional story line offer students the chance to see that authors make choices and that when you change a traditional story line, vocabulary becomes crucial. In *The House That Drac Built,* Judy Sierra draws on lots of bloodcurdling words when she peoples her house with a cast of creepies. In *The Lot at the End of My Block,* Kevin Lewis draws on the vocabulary of construction: "This is the shovel that backs with a beep / and fills the dump truck with dirt from the heap." It's a text that won't travel beyond first or second grade, but you can take the concept to older children, challenging them to try a construction format.

Your students will delight in the fact

Make a list of all the three-letter palindromes you can think of, such as words like *Mom* and *Pop* that read the same forward and backward. Once you have your list, try putting two or more of these words on a page in a palindrome sentence. Draw an illustration.

Challenge: Try to find four-letter palindromes.

Super Challenge: Can you find a five-letter palindrome?

that Simms Taback's award-winning version of *Old Lady* offers a traditional text but lots of innovative asides, such as where the line *There was an old lady who swallowed a spider* is accompanied by a recipe for spider's soup. And the aside for the line *There was an old lady who swallowed a bird* shows birds on a tree branch: *European tree sparrow, blue jay, Hungarian partridge, robin, magnolia warbler, scarlet tanager,* and so on. Before long, the reader is much more eager to read these asides than to be reminded of what the old lady swallowed next. The penultimate aside appears on the back of the dustjacket: Lots of flies, carefully labeled: *lauxanid fly, robber fly, syrphid fly, bee fly, deer fly, blow fly, dragon fly, tsetse fly, horse fly,* and so on.

In *There Was an Old Lady Who Swallowed a Trout!* Teri Sloat has her heroine ingesting not only a trout, but a salmon, an otter, a seal, and so on. In *I Know an Old Lady Who Swallowed a Pie,* Alison Jackson's use of the familiar structure teaches young readers that writers borrow from other writers. By making even small changes in someone else's story you can make a story of your own. In Jackson's text, the ravenous oldster comes to Thanksgiving dinner. First she swallows a pie, then a jug of cider, and so on:

> I know an old lady who swallowed a
>   salad
> She was looking quite pallid from eating
>   that salad.

Pallid. Once again we find out how children acquire voluminous vocabularies.

Read More

In *Too Hot to Hoot: Funny Palindrome Riddles,* Marvin Terban provides the link between palindromes and riddles. These start out easy, with a three-letter palindrome riddle: "What's a three-letter word for mother?" Next, come four-letter palindromes: the sound of a boat horn; a paper that shows you own property. Then the palindromes get harder still. And it's all about vocabulary.

Teaching Tip

Don't think you can't capitalize on this idea if you don't have the books. You can take the idea to students. What about *The Firehouse That Jill Built?* Or *The Athletic Arena That Jack Built?* Famed architect Robert Stern wrote *The House That Bob Built,* featuring a dream house by the sea, with lots of attention to architectural detail. How about using the format for building a yurta, a minaret, pagoda, or other interesting structure?

Reading Poems Kids Like to Grow a Vocabulary Garden

Not knowing where to start to present the case that popular poets provide incredible language lessons, I just walked into a bookstore and grabbed a book by my third graders' favorite

Word Watch

Challenge students to write a story about *The Old Lady Who Swallowed a Buttercup*—or a bluebonnet, lion's-ear, or whatever. How about a series of snakes? Purple foods? An alphabet of precious and semi-precious stones? To write such tales, students will have to research the topics and learn the vocabulary that goes with the territory. You can help them get started by using the *Garden of Flower Names* list of interesting flower names (see next page)—or send them off to gardening books to find their own names.

poet. From the time he is awakened by his rattlesnake until he goes to bed, bidding good night to silent vipers, tiny parasites, furtive spiders, loathsome vermin, and so on, Jack Prelutsky's *Awful Ogre's Awful Day* introduces readers to a world of verbal delight. There are plenty of words with obvious kid appeal—*buzzard, tarantula, piranha, scorpion,* and *lizard*—and Prelutsky also causes readers to stretch—with *disengage* and *besiege, perilous thorn, ramshackle patches,* and *blight-ridden pools.* "Awful Ogre and the Storm," to name just one poem, offers these delicious phrases:

- a legion of clouds in dark armor
- tentative raindrops
- ominous wind
- cascading in torrents
- retreat to their hovels
- glorious, glorious day

"Awful Ogre Dances" offers up *intricate, abandon, bravura, zest, carom, pirouette, panache,* and *unparalleled grace.* Paul Zelinsky's illustrations, which have panache and unparalleled grace themselves, will keep young readers on the page while these difficult words work their magic. Among the seventeen words of the short poem "Awful Ogre Speaks of Stature," young readers meet *encounter, grotesque, magnanimity,* and *statuesque.* And we're not even halfway through the book.

Bobbi Katz's *A Rumpus of Rhymes: A Book*

Read More

Diana Wells's *100 Flowers and How They Got Their Names* is a book written for adults. But from abelia to zinna, there is plenty of history, etymology, folk belief, and stories here to share with children. In learning about how flowers got their names, children will also learn about ambitious explorers, clever hucksters, imperious monarchs, and persevering scientists. They'll learn that Thomas Jefferson planted nasturtiums every year, hoping to get enough seeds for a bed of nasturtiums ten by nineteen yards. And they'll learn that nasturtiums, flowers originating in South America, were first described in 1569 by the Spanish physician and plant collector Nicholas Monardes. Their name comes from the Latin *nasus,* meaning *nose,* and *tortus,* meaning *twisted,* because their pungent smell makes one's nose wrinkle or twist.

of Noises definitely delivers on the subtitle. Along with *hush, whoosh,* and *whisper,* the reader gets *CLANK, CLUNK, CRASH, CHINETY-CHONKETY, SNORT, BELLOW, THUMP, YODDLE, SHRIEK, ROAR,* and *KERPLOP!* Not to mention *glubita glubita, babba-da-swaba,* and *blub-blub-a-dubba.* Don't know what these words mean? You will when you read the book. The poems are short, noisy, and fun. In their wonderful display of onomatopoeia, they offer readers a ringside seat on verbal virtuosity and beg these readers to try some verbal antics of their own.

The first rainy day in the fall produced lots of mud, which meant lots of opportunity for third-grade fun. I read a few mud poems, ones like Zilpha Keatley Snyder's "Poem to Mud," that had mudlucious words:

There's nothing sloppier, slipperier,
  floppier,
There's nothing slickier, stickier, thickier,
There's nothing quickier to make grown-
  ups sickier.

And Polly Chase Boyden's "Mud," with the line "Mud is very nice to feel / All squishy-squash between the toes!"

A Garden of Flower Names

Directions

Pick your favorite flower names from this list, and then follow your teacher's suggestions for more learning fun.

baby's breath	cuckoo-bud	mosquito trap
bachelor's button	cup-and-saucer	mouse-ear
black-eyed Susan	daisy	pocketbook plant
blazing star	dandelion	Queen Anne's lace
bleeding heart	devil's paintbrush	rattlesnake master
blue bonnet	devil's tongue	rocket larkspur
blue-eyed grass	dogtooth violet	skunkweed
boneset	dogwood	sleepy dick
buffalo berry	Dutchman's-breeches	sneezeweed
butter-and-eggs	Dutchman's pipe	Spanish dagger
buttercup	elephant-ear fern	spider lily
butterfly weed	fleabane	sunflower
candytuft	forget-me-not	sweet william catchfly
cattail	Indian blanket	tiger lily
Cherokee rose	jack-in-the-pulpit	trout lily
Chinese houses	Johnny-jump-up	trumpet honeysuckle
chocolate flower	lady's slipper	turtlehead
coffeeweed	lion's-ear	wild pink snapdragon
cowslip	liverleaf	witchweed
crowtoe	milkweed	yellow loosestrife

© 2002 by Susan Ohanian from *The Great Word Catalogue: FUNdamental Activities for Building Vocabulary*. Portsmouth, NH: Heinemann.

Teaching Tips

"There's a flower for every mood of the mind," noted Henry David Thoreau in his journal on June 25, 1852. There's probably one for every mood of the classroom too. Certainly, flower names have lots of possibilities for engaging students in vocabulary study. Encourage students to enjoy the very sound of the names. Then challenge them to establish categories, using whatever rules they wish.

■ Encourage students to investigate how the iris, amaryllis, hyacinth, delphinium, and narcissus got their names. They can also investigate William Forsyth, Joel Poinsett, Louis Antoine de Bougainville, George Joseph Kamel, Casper Wister, and Lysimachus, and the flowers which bear their names. Then students can invent a naming story for one of the flowers on the list.

■ A line from Natalia Belting's poem "Our Fathers Had Powerful Songs" offers provocative research material for young readers: "The women cease gathering milkweed for twine." In finding out the uses of milkweed, students will learn some history and will also learn that poetry is often "factual."

■ There is plenty of metaphor in flower names. The iris provides a wonderful introduction to metaphor. After students have looked at pictures of these colorful flowers, ask them to guess why the iris, a thing of the earth, is named for the goddess of the rainbow.

■ Mother Goose provides metaphor mixed with wordplay for readers of all ages to savor.

> Daffadowndilly
> Has come to town
> In a yellow petticoat
> And a green gown.

■ Encourage students to play with flower names. They can try their hand at writing floral tongue twisters. And nobody has yet written a flower riddle book. Challenge your students to become the first.

Invite students to ponder other provocative mind pictures. Howard Nemerov calls dandelions "these common suns." Aileen Fisher says "Our lawn has a jacket . . . with many more buttons / than jackets should hold." For Myra Cohn Livingston, "hollyhocks twirl around / like dancing ladies' skirts."

To help students understand that many flower names are themselves metaphors, encourage them to draw zany pictures based on a literal interpretation of the flowers' names. David McCord's "Spring Talk" can show the way, both delighting your students and helping to unleash their own creative juices with such fun as "Well, dogtooth violet, and how's that tooth?"

We wrote about mud in class. Steve offered:

> Mud is Yucky
> Squishy
> Mushy
> Gushy
> Yummy!

Jessica, one of the sweetest, gentlest, most helpful students in the class offered this one. Picking up on *squishy* from Boyden and *yucky* from Steve, she then added her own special interpretation:

> Mud is yucky.
> Mud is squishy.
> Mud is like puke.
> But sometimes . . .
> Mud is yummy like chocolate pie.

Her classmates asked me, "You aren't going to type up *that* word are you?"

"Why not?" I answered. "Isn't it part of her poem? It's called a simile, comparing one thing with another. It's something poets do."

Students seemed especially eager to take home the read-aloud homework that night. I was glad this linguistic breakthrough happened so early in the year, letting kids know that they could play with words and even use a few highly charged words, like *puke*. I was especially glad it was Jessica's idea. Feeling

Read More

Try reading Karel Capek's *The Gardener's Year* aloud in the faculty room. First published in 1931 and recently reissued, the book's fans range from Arthur Miller to John Updike. Books don't get funnier—or better written—than this one. And the parallels of tending a garden and tending a classroom are obvious.

unworthy because she was repeating third grade, this shy, soft-spoken child needed and deserved her dance in the limelight, showing off her derring-do.

We were in a school where so-called language rules were fiercely enforced. Next door there were posters on the wall:

- Never begin a sentence with "And."
- Never begin a sentence with "Because."

Never do this. Never do that. What a view of language these "Nevers" presented. So I was always on the lookout for made-up words, hoping to prod my students into becoming word inventors too. Joseph was very much bothered by Snyder's *sickier*. "That's not a word!" he complained. I replied, "That's the joy of being a poet. Poets can do anything they want with words."

Three months later we wrote celery poems in response to Ogden Nash's little verse on this subject. I confess I have a strange fondness for Bryant's contribution:

> Celery is like my sister's cookies—
> bitter
> sour
> hard
> tough
> and etc.

Bryant did not offer this as a funny poem, just as a description of the facts of life.

Here's Joseph's poem:

> Celery is crunchy.
> And comes in a bunchy.

Very seriously, Joseph pronounced, "Poets can do anything they want with words."

The delight of our sacred calling is that the words and deeds we offer children come back to us.

References

Adult Books

Ammer, Christine. *The American Heritage Dictionary of Idioms.* (Houghton Mifflin 1997).

———. *Seeing Red or Tickled Pink: Color Terms in Everyday Language.* (Dutton 1992).

Brandreth, Gyles. *The Joy of Lex: How to Have Fun with 860,341,500 Words.* (Morrow 1980).

Brock, Suzanne. *Idiom's Delight.* (Times Books 1988).

Capek, Karel. *The Gardner's Year.* (Modern Library 2002).

Crystal, David. *Language Play.* (University of Chicago 1998).

Davies, Christopher. *Divided by a Common Language.* (Mayflower Press 1997).

Dickson, Paul. *Slang.* (Pocket Books 1998).

Donner, Michael. *I Love Me, Vol. I.* (Algonquin Books 1996).

Dunn, Jerry. *Idiom Savant: Slang as It Is Slung.* (Henry Holt 1997).

Espy, Willard. *Another Almanac of Words at Play.* (Clarkson N. Potter 1980).

———. *The Game of Words.* (Random House 1972).

———. *The Word's Gotten Out: A Commonplace Book.* (Clarkson N. Potter 1989).

Farb, Peter. *Word Play: What Happens When People Talk.* (Knopf 1974, 1993).

Geller, Linda Gibson. *Word Play and Language Learning for Children.* (National Council of Teachers of English 1985).

Hendrickson, Robert. *Happy Trails: A Dictionary of Western Expressions.* (Facts on File 1994).

———. *QPB Encyclopedia of Word and Phrase Origins.* (Facts on File 1997).

Hobbs, James B. *Homophones and Homographs: An American Dictionary.* (McFarland 1986).

Isil, Olivia A. *When a Loose Cannon Flogs a Dead Horse There's the Devil to Pay.* (International Marine 1996).

Kacirk, Jeffrey. *Forgotten English.* (Morrow 1997).

———. *The Word Museum: The Most Remarkable English Words Ever Forgotten.* (Touchstone 2000).

Lederer, Richard. *Word Circus.* (Merriam-Webster 1998).

Lewin, Esther and Albert E. Lewin. *The Thesaurus of Slang.* (Facts on File 1997).

Mieder, Wolfgang. *Proverbs Are Never Out of Season: Popular Wisdom in the Modern Age.* (Oxford 1993).

Mieder, Wolfgang and Alan Dundes (eds.). *The Wisdom of Many: Essays on the Proverb.* (Garland 1981).

Meider, Wolfgang and Deborah Holmes. *Children and Proverbs Speak the Truth: Teaching Proverbial Wisdom to Fourth Graders.* (University of Vermont 2000).

Morris, Evan. *The Word Detective.* (Algonquin 2000).

Raswon, Hugh. *Devious Derivations.* (Crown 1994).

Rosenthal, Peggy and George Dardess. *Every Cliché in the Book.* (Morrow 1987).

Wells, Diana. *100 Birds and How They Got Their Names.* (Algonquin 2002).

———. *100 Flowers and How They Got Their Names.* (Algonquin 1997).

Children's Books

Ackerman, Karen. *Flannery Row: An Alphabetic Rhyme.* (Atlantic Monthly 1986).

Ada, Alma Flor. *Gathering the Sun: An Alphabet in Spanish and English.* (Lothrop, Lee & Shepard 1997).

Adler, David A. *The Dinosaur Princess and Other Prehistoric Riddles.* (Holiday House 1988).

———. *Remember Betsy Floss and Other Colonial American Riddles.* (Holiday House 1987).

Agee, Jon. *Elvis Lives! and Other Anagrams.* (Farrar, Straus, Giroux 2000).

———. *Go Hang a Salami! I'm a Lasagna Hog!* (Farrar, Straus, Giroux 1991).

———. *Sit on a Potato Pan, Otis! More Palindromes.* (Farrar, Straus, Giroux 1999).

———. *So Many Dynamos!* (Farrar, Straus, Giroux 1994).

———. *Who Ordered the Jumbo Shrimp? and Other Oxymorons.* (Farrar, Straus, Giroux 1998).

Arnold, Tim. *Natural History from A to Z: A Terrestrial Sampler.* (Margaret K. McElderry/Macmillan 1991).

Azarian, Mary. *A Farmer's Alphabet.* (Godine 1981).

Barron, Rex. *Fed Up! A Feast of Frazzled Foods.* (Putnam 2000).

Belting, Natalia. *Our Fathers Had Powerful Songs.* (Dutton 1974).

Bernstein, Joanne E. and Paul Cohen. *Creepy Crawly Critter Riddles.* (Albert Whitman 1986).

Borlenghi, Patricia. *From Albatross to Zoo.* (Scholastic 1992).

Boyden, Polly Chase. "Mud" in *The Random House Book of Poetry for Children,* selected by Jack Prelutsky. (Random House 1983).

Brown, Marcia. *Peter Piper's Alphabet.* (Scribner 1959).

Carter, Angela. *Comic and Curious Cats.* (Random House 1979).

Chess, Victoria. *Alfred's Alphabet Walk.* (Greenwillow 1979).

Clements, Andrew. *Double Trouble in Walla Walla*. (Millbrook 1997).

Cole, Joanna and Stephanie Calmenson. *Why Did the Chicken Cross the Road? And Other Riddles Old and New*. (Morrow 1994).

Dragonwagon, Crescent. *Alligator Arrived with Apples: A Potluck Alphabet Feast*. (Aladdin 1992).

Eichenberg, Fritz. *Ape in a Cape*. (Harcourt 1989).

Elting, Mary. *Q Is for Duck: An Alphabet Guessing Game*. (Houghton Mifflin 1985).

Eschbacher, Roger. *Nonsense! He Yelled*. (Dial 2002).

Farber, Norma. *As I Was Crossing Boston Common*. (Dutton 1973).

Fisher, Leonard E. *Alphabet Art: Thirteen ABCs from Around the World*. (Scholastic 1978).

Florian, Douglas. *Bing Bang Boing*. (Harcourt Brace 1994).

———. *Insectology*. (Harcourt Brace 1998).

———. *In the Swim*. (Harcourt Brace 1997).

———. *Laugh-eteria*. (Harcourt Brace 1999).

———. *Lizards, Frogs, and Polliwogs*. (Harcourt Brace 2001).

Folsom, Marcia and Michael. *Easy as Pie: A Guessing Game of Sayings*. (Clarion 1985).

Gackenbach, Dick. *Supposes*. (Harcourt 1991).

Goldstone, Bruce. *The Beastly Feast*. (Henry Holt 1998).

Graham, Joan Bransfield. *Splish Splash*. (Houghton Mifflin 1994).

Grossman, Bill. *My Little Sister Ate One Hare*. (Crown 1996).

Grover, Max. *The Accidental Zucchini: An Unexpected Alphabet*. (Harcourt 1997).

———. *Max's Wacky Taxi Day*. (Harcourt 1997).

Gwynne, Fred. *A Chocolate Moose for Dinner*. (Simon & Schuster 1976).

———. *The King Who Rained*. (Simon & Schuster 1988).

———. *A Little Pigeon-Toad*. (Simon & Schuster 1988).

———. *The Sixteen Hand Horse*. (Simon & Schuster 1980).

Hall, Katy and Lisa Eisenberg. *Batty Riddles*. (Dial).

———. *Buggy Riddles*. (Dial 1986).

———. *Bunny Riddles*. (Dial 1997).

———. *Chickey Riddles*. (Dial 1997).

———. *Creepy Riddles*. (Dial 1998).

———. *Dino Riddles*. (Dial 2002).

———. *Fishy Riddles*. (Dial 1989).

———. *Grizzly Riddles*. (Dial 1989).

———. *Kitty Riddles*. (Dial 2000).

———. *Mummy Riddles*. (Dial 1997).

———. *Puppy Riddles*. (Dial 1998).

———. *Sheepish Riddles*. (Dial 1996).

———. *Snakey Riddles*. (Dial 1994).

———. *Spacey Riddles*. (Dial 1992).

Heck, Joseph. *Dinosaur Riddles*. (Julian Messner 1982).

Heller, Nicholas. *Goblins in Green*. (Greenwillow 1995).

———. *Ogres! Ogres! Ogres! A Feasting Frenzy from A to Z*. (Greenwillow 1999).

Hepworth, Cathi. *Antics!* (Putnam 1992).

———. *Bug Off!* (Putnam 1998).

Holman, Felice. *The Song in My Head and Other Poems*. (Scribner 1985).

Hymes, Lucia and James L. *Oodles of Noodles*. (Addison-Wesley 1964).

Jackson, Alison. *I Know an Old Lady Who Swallowed a Pie*. (Dutton 1997).

Jeffares, Jeanne. *An Around-the-World Alphabet Book*. (Peter Bedrick 1989).

Jonas, Ann. *Aardvarks, Disembark!* (Greenwillow 1990).

Juster, Norton. *The Phantom Tollbooth*. (Random House 1988).

———. *A Surfeit of Similes*. (Morrow 1989). (Revised as *As Silly As Knees, As Busy As Bees: An Astounding Assortment of Similes*. Beech Tree Books 1998).

Katz, Bobbi. *Rumpus of Rhymes: A Book of Noisy Poems*. (Dutton 2001).

Kennedy, X. J. *Ghastlies, Goops, and Pincushions*. (Macmillan 1989).

Lewis, J. Patrick. *Good Mousekeeping and Other Animal Home Poems*. (Atheneum 2001).

———. *A Hippopotamusn't*. (Dial 1990).

Lewis, Kevin. *The Lot at the End of My Block*. (Hyperion 2001).

Lobel, Anita. *Alison's Zinnia*. (Greenwillow 1990).

———. *Away from Home*. (Greenwillow 1994).

Lyon, George Ella. *A Day at Damp Camp*. (Orchard 1996).

Maddex, Diane (ed.). *Built in the USA: American Buildings from Airports to Zoos*. (Preservation 1985).

Maestro, Giulio. *Riddle Roundup: A Wild Bunch to Beef Up Your Word Power!* (Clarion 1989).

———. *Macho Nacho and Other Rhyming Riddles*. (Dutton 1994).

———. *What's Mite Might? Homophone Riddles to Boost Your World Power!* (Clarion 1986).

Mauer, Donna. *Annie, Bea, and Chi Chi Dolores: A School Day Alphabet*. (Orchard 1993).

McCord, David. *One at a Time*. (Little, Brown 1974).

McCurdy, Michael. *The Sailor's Alphabet*. (Houghton Mifflin 1998).

McMillan, Bruce. *One Sun: A Book of Terse Verse*. (Holiday House 1992).

———. *Play Day: A Book of Terse Verse*. (Holiday House 1991).

Miles, Miska. *Apricot ABC*. (Atlantic/Little, Brown 1969).

Most, Bernard. *Happy Holidaysaurus!* (Harcourt Brace 1992).

———. *If the Dinosaurs Came Back*. (Harcourt Brace 1978).

———. *Moo-Ha!* (Harcourt Brace 1997).

———. *There's an Ant in Anthony*. (Mulberry 1992).

Mullins, Patricia. *V for Vanishing*. (HarperCollins 1993).

Musgrove, Margaret. *Ashanti to Zulu: African Traditions*. (Dial 1977).

Paul, Ann Whitford. *Eight Hands Round: A Patchwork Alphabet*. (HarperCollins 1991).

Phillips, Louis. *Invisible Oink: Pig Jokes*. (Viking 1993).

———. *Wackysaurus Dinosaur Jokes*. (Viking 1991).

Poulin, Stephanie. *Ah! Belle Cité!/A Beautiful City ABC*. (Tundra 1985).

Prelutsky, Jack. *Awful Ogre's Awful Day*. (Greenwillow 2001).

Reed, Lynn Rowe. *Pedro, His Perro, and the Alphabet Sombrero*. (Hyperion 1995).

Rice, James. *Cajun Alphabet*. (Pelican 1976).

Roberts, Michael. *The Jungle ABC*. (Callaway/Hyperion 1998).

———. *Mumbo Jumbo: The Creepy ABC*. (Callaway/Hyperion 2000).

Scieszka, John. *The Book That Jack Wrote*. (Viking 1994).

Shannon, George. *Tomorrow's Alphabet*. (Greenwillow 1996).

Shelby, Anne. *Potluck*. (Orchard 1991).

Sierra, Judy. *The House That Drac Built*. (Harcourt Brace 1995).

Silverstein, Shel. *Who Wants a Cheap Rhinoceros?* (Simon & Schuster 1983).

Sloat, Teri. *There Was an Old Lady Who Swallowed a Trout!* (Henry Holt 1998).

Snow, Alan. *The Monster Book of ABC Sounds*. (Dial 1991).

Snyder, Zilpha Keatley. "Poem to Mud" in *The 20th Century Children's Poetry Treasury*. Selected by Jack Prelutsky. (Knopf 1999).

Steig, Jeanne and William. *Alpha Beta Chowder*. (Harper 1992).

Stern, Robert. *The House That Bob Built*. (Rizzoli 1991).

Taback, Simms. *There Was an Old Lady Who Swallowed a Fly*. (Viking 1997).

Terban, Marvin. *The Dove Dove: Funny Homograph Riddles*. (Clarion 1988).

———. *Eight Ate: A Feast of Homonym Riddles*. (Clarion 1982).

———. *Funny You Should Ask: How to Make Up Jokes and Riddles with Wordplay*. (Clarion 1992).

———. *In a Pickle and Other Funny Idioms*. (Clarion 1983).

———. *It Figures! Fun Figures of Speech*. (Clarion 1993).

———. *Mad as a Wet Hen! and Other Funny Idioms*. (Clarion 1987).

———. *Punching the Clock: Funny Action Idioms*. (Clarion 1990).

———. *Scholastic Dictionary of Idioms*. (Scholastic 1998).

———. *Too Hot to Hoot: Funny Palindrome Riddles*. (Clarion 1985).

———. *What's a Frank Frank? Tasty Homograph Riddles*. (Clarion 1984).

Venokur, Ross. *The Amazing Frecktackle*. (Yearling 2000).

Wilbur, Richard. *The Disappearing Alphabet*. (Harcourt Brace 1998).

Wilson, Ron. *100 Dinosaurs from A to Z*. (Grosset & Dunlap 1986).

Zabar, Abbie. *Alphabet Soup*. (Stewart, Tabori & Chang 1990).

APPENDIX
Words in Context Bank

In his spare time Joshua read all he could about the science of celestial navigation and practiced with the sextant, the instrument used for locating a ship's position on the sea by measuring the angles between the stars and the horizon.
—*Born in the Breezes: The Seafaring Life of Joshua Slocum*, Kathryn Lasky

Sylvia is my goldfish. I'm fond of her, but let's face it. She's not cuddly. She can't chase a ball or a piece of string. She can't sleep at the foot of my bed. And she can't really comfort me when I'm lonely or sad. It's not her fault. She just doesn't have what you could call a sympathetic manner.
—*Albertina, the Animals, and Me*, Susi Gregg Fowler

Helen's family became worried when it seemed that their daughter had become too zealous in her pursuit of knowledge. They fretted when she would rather finger-spell than eat.
—*Helen Keller, Rebellious Spirit*, Laurie Lawlor

The Mole waggled his toes from sheer happiness, spread his chest with a sigh of full contentment, and leaned back blissfully into the soft cushions.
—*The Wind in the Willows*, Kenneth Grahame

For thousands of years, scientists could only guess what Earth was like inside. But in 1880, the English engineer John Milne created an invention that was to unlock Earth's hidden structure. This invention, the seismograph, senses vibrations in Earth caused by earthquakes. It reveals facts about Earth's interior because the speed of an earthquake vibration, called a seismic wave, changes when it goes through different types of material.
—*Shake, Rattle, and Roll: The World's Most Amazing Earthquakes, Volcanoes, and Other Forces*, Spencer Christian

"An immensely complex spell," he said squeakily, "involving the magical concealment of a secret inside a single, living soul. The information is hidden inside the chosen person, or Secret-Keeper, and is henceforth impossible to find—unless, of course, the Secret-Keeper chooses to divulge it."

—*Harry Potter and the Prisoner of Azkaban*, J. K. Rowling

Babar then buys himself: a shirt with a collar and tie, a suit of a becoming shade of green, then a handsome derby hat, and also shoes with spats.

   Well satisfied with his purchases and feeling very elegant indeed, Babar now goes to the photographer to have his picture taken.

—*Babar*, Jean de Brunhoff

[The narrator of this passage is a mouse, who is writing about the poet Emily Dickinson.] It must have been Fate that steered me to choose Emily's bedroom for my own. My proximity gave me a chance to observe her closely.

—*The Mouse of Amherst*, Elizabeth Spires

High above the city, on a tall column, stood the statue of the Happy Prince. He was gilded all over with thin leaves of fine gold, for eyes he had two bright sapphires, and a large red ruby glowed on his sword-hilt.

—"The Happy Prince," Oscar Wilde

For a long time [the velveteen rabbit] lived in the toy cupboard or on the nursery floor, and no one thought very much about him. He was naturally shy, and since he was only made of velveteen, some of the more expensive toys quite snubbed him.

—*The Velveteen Rabbit*, Margery Williams

In 1066, Normans from France won the Battle of Hastings, conquering the Anglo-Saxons.

—*The Journey of English*, Donna Brook

Ben worked hard to bring about all these civic improvements. He served on countless committees and wrote one newspaper article after another. But he always played down his own role in the proceedings. For he had learned that people were more likely to endorse something new if they thought it was their idea.

—*The Amazing Life of Benjamin Franklin*, James Cross Giblin

Many years ago there was an emperor who was so excessively fond of new clothes that he spent all his money on them. He cared nothing about his soldiers, nor for the theater, nor for driving in the woods except for the sake of showing off his new clothes. He had a costume for every hour in the day.

—"The Emperor's New Clothes," Hans Christian Andersen

When the boat was finished, he loaded it with cheese, biscuits, acorns, honey, wheat germ, two barrels of fresh water, a compass, a sextant, a telescope, a saw, a hammer and nails and some wood in case repairs should be necessary, a needle and thread for the mending of torn sails, and various other necessities such as bandages and iodine, a yo-yo and playing cards.

—*Amos & Boris*, William Steig

Mr. Crinkley buried his nose in the book again. He was a very fast reader. Milo watched him raise his eyebrows and wrinkle his nose and scratch his ear as he scanned the pages. Then Mr. Crinkley shut the book and laid it back on the desk.

—*Be a Perfect Person in Just Three Days!* Stephen Manes

Harry's euphoria at finally winning the Quidditch Cup lasted a week. Even the weather seemed to be celebrating.

—*Harry Potter and the Prisoner of Azkaban*, J. K. Rowling

There were about one hundred fifty kids in fifth grade. And there were seven fifth-grade teachers: two math, two science, two social studies, but only one language arts teacher. In language arts, Mrs. Granger had a monopoly—and a reputation.

—*Frindle*, Andrew Clements

One day in the early 1800s a tidal wave crashed down on the shores of Cape Cod in New England. After the wave had washed back out to sea, the villagers heard deep, bellowing sounds coming from the beach. When they rushed to find out what was going on, they couldn't believe their eyes. A giant baby three fathoms tall—or eighteen feet!—was crawling across the sand, crying in a voice as loud as a foghorn.

—*American Tall Tales*, Mary Pope Osborne

I shall never forget the first time I laid these now tired old eyes on our visitor. I had been left home by the family with the admonition to take care of the house until they returned. That's something they always say to me when they go out: "Take care of the house, Harold. You're the watchdog."

—*Bunnicula*, Deborah Howe and James Howe

Pochontas kept telling herself that she'd be a captive for only a short time. As soon as her father was told what had happened, he'd do whatever he had to do to free her.

—*The Double Life of Pocahontas*, Jean Fritz

After some nine months of planning, the White House was completely gutted. Not a floor was kept. Only its original stone walls were left standing. Much of the historic interior was removed and crated for future reassembly.

—*The White House*, Leonard Everett Fisher

Beneath this was a picture of a big-bellied, crocodile-faced sea dragon calmly biting a giant squid in two. My first thought on seeing this carnage was, "What big teeth he has!"

—*The Great Whale of Kansas*, Richard W. Jennings

Other Arizona wonders include cactuses that grow as tall as six-story buildings, and the eerie, leafless Petrified Forest. The "forest's" fallen, decayed trees—over a hundred million years old—lie on the ground in broken pieces that have petrified, or gradually turned to colored stone.

—*It Happened in America: True Stories from the Fifty States*, Lila Perl

As the narrator tells us, by his own reckoning and that of everyone else, they were supposed to be thirty-five leagues, about a hundred miles, from land. The word "reckoning" was short for "dead reckoning"—the system used by ships at sea to keep track of their position, meaning their longitude and latitude. It was an intricate system, a craft, and like every other craft involved the mastery of certain tools, in this case such instruments as compass, hourglass, and quadrant. It was an art as well.

—*The Longitude Prize*, Joan Dash

Every great detective should have an admiring friend and biographer who is able to record exploits, feats of mental brilliance and acts of bravery. It sounds like bragging when the detective is forced to write about herself.

—*The Disappearance of Sister Perfect*, Jill Pinkwater

When a chief decided to have a potlatch, he counted his possessions—his canoes, his blankets, his dentalium (shell money), and everything else he owned. He called a tallyman to help him keep track of how many gifts he could give to each guest. If he did not think he had enough property for everyone, he asked family members to help him make extra things. At the potlatch he would give away nearly everything he owned.

—*Brown Paper School U.S. Kids' History: Book of the American Indians*,
Marlene Smith Baranzini and Howard Egger-Bovet

Sidney Lanier denounced the bureaucratic decision to imprison the Indians in the old Spanish fort, which he said was "as unfit for them as they for it."
—*A Strange and Distant Shore: Indians of the Great Plains in Exile*, Brent Ashabranner

He smiled and so did she, for she then felt more certain than ever that she had chosen both the correct brother for a partner in escape. They complemented each other perfectly. She was cautious (about everything but money) and poor; he was adventurous (about everything but money) and rich.

—*From the Mixed-Up Files of Mrs. Basil E. Frankweiler*, E. L. Konigsburg

"Do you have an extra pencil? I can't find mine."
   Howie Wolfner, the boy next to Danny, shook his head and a strand of his thick reddish brown hair fell into his eyes. He pushed it back with one hand and said, "Afraid not, chum. Have you rifled the empty desk next to you?"

—*The Monster in Creeps Head Bay*, Mel Gilden

More provisions coming on, bread, fresh Beef, Mutton, Salt, Wheat.

—*Stowaway*, Karen Hesse

In mid-April small flocks of the unnamed bird began their yearly migration north. The striking black-and-yellow-headed males had recently begun to sing. For several days they and the olive-crowned females had been eating ravenously, storing fat to fuel their journey.

—*Townsend's Warbler*, Paul Fleischman

My grandfather kept his ties in a tall cherrywood chifforobe . . . He called the chifforobe "Jeeves," after a character is some books he liked; he said he couldn't get dressed without Jeeves, and it was true. Jeeves held his four or five suits in a tall compartment for hangers, his shirts and socks in smoothly worn drawers, and his jewelry in a built-in bird's-eye maple box lined with the spruce-green felt. But the chifforobe's best feature was a collapsible nickel tie rack that folded out from the inside of its left-hand door, to offer my grandfather his fabulous array of silk bow ties.

—*Everywhere*, Bruce Brooks

"All the many names of the Supreme Being—God, Jehovah, Allah, and so on—they are only man-made labels. There is a philosophical problem of some difficulty here, which I do not propose to discuss, but somewhere among all the possible combinations of letters which can occur are what one may call the real names of God. By systematic permutation of letters, we have been trying to list them all."

"I see. You've been starting at AAAAAAAAA . . . and working up to ZZZZZZZZZ . . ."

—"The Nine Billion Names of God," Arthur C. Clarke

Prince Raphael was as rich and handsome as a prince should be. His father had assembled scholars from all over the world to teach him, so he was highly educated. The people should have been proud to have Raphael as their next king, but instead they were afraid.

"Look at his eyes," they said, "and see the arrogance of a man who admires only himself."

"Look at his mouth," they said, "and see the sneer of a man who thinks everyone else is stupid."

"Look at his hands," they said, "and see the grasp of a man who thinks everyone else's goods are his for the taking."

—*The King's Equal*, Katherine Paterson

The word Holocaust means "destruction by fire" and has come to refer specifically to one of the darkest chapters in history, to when, over a period of more than four years, one nation and its leader, Nazi Germany and Adolf Hitler, tried by all possible means to exterminate the entire Jewish population of Europe—and almost succeeded. The numbers are staggering: There were eight million Jews, and six million of them (approximately the entire population of the state of Massachusetts) were murdered. Among these were one and a half million children who were under the age of sixteen when the war began in 1939.

—*After the Holocaust*, Howard Greenfield

Now comes the task of incubating the eggs, keeping them warm and dry. To do this job, penguins have a special pocket of bare skin called a brook pouch. Usually the breast muscles press the two sides of the pouch together, sealing it shut. During the incubation period, though, the parent relaxes these muscles to open the pouch. Warm blood flowing through the bare skin in the pouch warms the eggs.

—*Growing Up Wild: Penguins*, Sandra Markle